A Green Fingers Guide

VEGETABLES

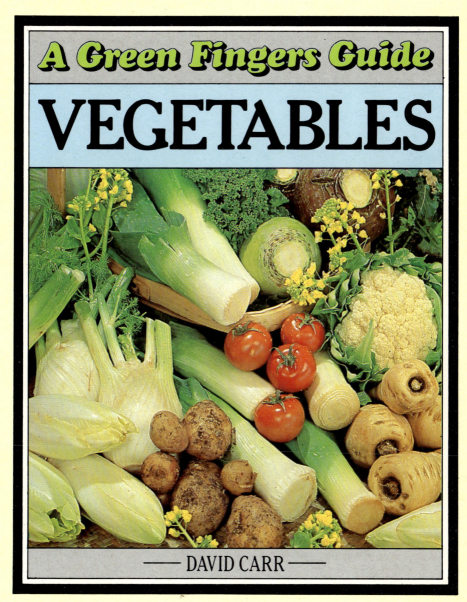

DAVID CARR

EBURY PRESS

Preparing the Ground

Thorough soil preparation is essential if bumper crops of good quality, size and flavour are to result. Whatever the natural variations in soil, ranging from light sands to heavy clay and including those of a peaty or a chalky nature, the main aim remains the same for all of them. It is to modify ground conditions to suit the needs of the individual crops for food, moisture, light and space. The chief preparatory operations are weedkilling, provision of adequate drainage, levelling, breaking up compacted soil, improving the texture by manuring and liming, and providing food by adding fertilizer. The timing of soil cultivation is important too and the goal should be to have completed the preparations to create the right soil conditions by the time of sowing and planting specific crops. Carry out deep cultivations, like digging, early, to allow the soil time to settle, before carrying out detailed tasks, such as seedbed preparations.

SOIL TREATMENT

The first step on vacant land is to fork out and remove the weeds. Badly weed-infested ground can be cleared using weedkiller, but avoid injury to nearby plants and allow time for harmful residues to disappear before sowing and planting – this can take up to six months. Drain wet ground, either by means of a simple rubble-filled sump or, on medium to large sites, by using drain pipes. Carry out double-digging or ridging for deep-rooted crops in the autumn. Single-digging, 30 cm (12 in) deep, using a spade or fork, is similar to double-digging but without forking up the trench bottom. It can be carried out at any time when the land is not waterlogged, frozen or bone dry. Allow time for settlement after digging. Pre-sowing cultivation is discussed later. These basic preparations are usually accompanied by manuring (see pages 8–9).

SOIL DRAINAGE

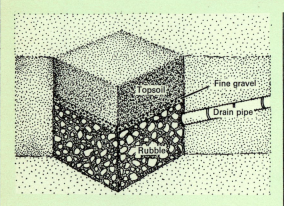

A rubble-filled hole can provide an effective and inexpensive method of draining small areas up to 4 m (13 ft) across. Site the sump drains in the lowest position possible.

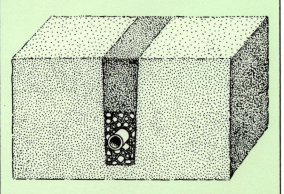

Plastic or porous clay pipes are necessary to drain medium to large sized areas. The pipes should run downhill to discharge at the lowest point into an outlet ditch or large sump.

PREPARATION FOR DEEP-ROOTED CROPS

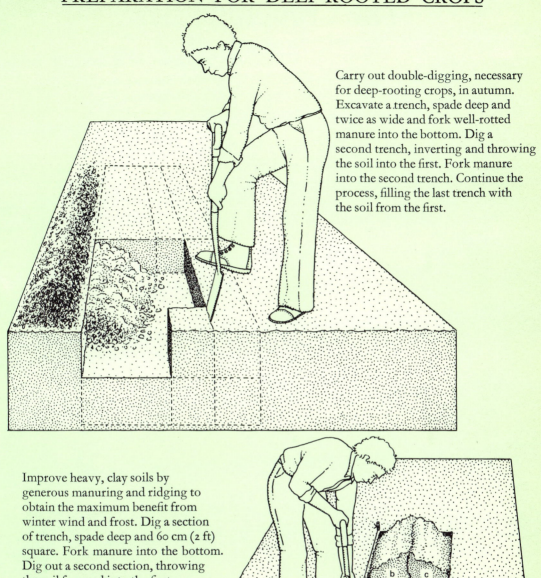

Carry out double-digging, necessary for deep-rooting crops, in autumn. Excavate a trench, spade deep and twice as wide and fork well-rotted manure into the bottom. Dig a second trench, inverting and throwing the soil into the first. Fork manure into the second trench. Continue the process, filling the last trench with the soil from the first.

Improve heavy, clay soils by generous manuring and ridging to obtain the maximum benefit from winter wind and frost. Dig a section of trench, spade deep and 60 cm (2 ft) square. Fork manure into the bottom. Dig out a second section, throwing the soil forward into the first. Repeat the process until one strip is ridged. Make adjoining ridges as required.

The Cropping Plan

A SIMPLE cropping plan can help gardeners choose and grow the crops which are in greatest demand, are difficult to obtain or are costly, and so make profitable use of garden space. The labour-saving advantages are considerable, especially in medium to large sized gardens. For example, by dividing the plot into four strips, 1–4, and the vegetables into four groups, A–D, the maximum benefit of double-digging can be obtained by deep-working strips 1–3 one year in three, shown opposite. Cost, time and effort can be saved by manuring each strip every three years, that is, manure for the pod and stem vegetables; the succeeding root and green crops utilize the residues. One of the biggest benefits of crop rotation is continued heavy cropping while still avoiding soil sickness. Each group of crops is grown on a different strip each year, within the three year period, discouraging the build up of pests and diseases.

PLANNING IN PRACTICE

First of all, decide which crops to grow and divide them into four groups as shown opposite. Mark out the vegetable plot into four strips, one for long-term crops and the other three, of equal size, for rotation purposes. In year 1, strip 1 should be double-dug and manured – this will apply successively to strips 2 and 3 in the two following years. Maximize the use of cloches within good rotation planning.

STRIP CROPPING WITH CLOCHES

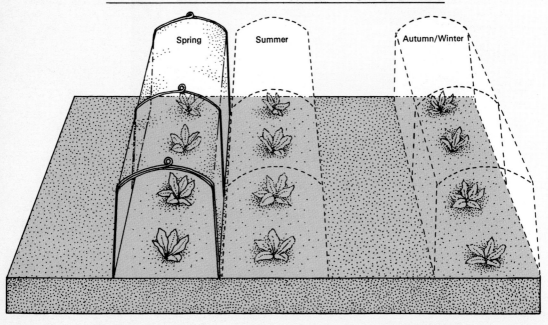

In spring, cover the strip of earliest crops with cloches. Move these on to adjoining strips of vegetables as they mature. This allows the maximum use of cover with the minimum of effort.

CROPS GROUPING

Group A Pod and Stem

Beans, Broad, Dwarf French and Runner

Celery

Cucumber, Ridge

Lamb's Lettuce or Corn Salad

Leeks

Lettuce

Marrow and Courgettes

Onions and Shallots

Peas

Spinach

Sweetcorn

Tomato (Outdoors)

Group B Roots

Artichoke, Jerusalem

Beetroot

Carrot

Parsnips

Potatoes

Swede and Turnip

Group C Greens

Broccoli, Sprouting

Brussels Sprouts

Cabbage and Savoy

Cauliflower

Group D Permanent

Artichoke, Globe

Asparagus

Herbs

Container/Greenhouse

Cucumber

Marrow and Courgettes

Peppers

Tomatoes (Greenhouse)

ROTATION – CROP SUCCESSION

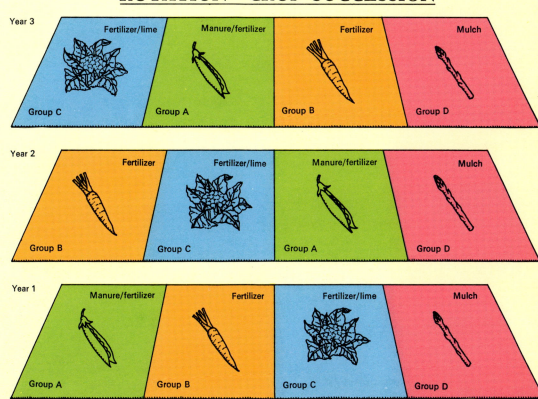

Year 3

| Group C | Group A | Group B | Group D |
| Fertilizer/lime | Manure/fertilizer | Fertilizer | Mulch |

Year 2

| Group B | Group C | Group A | Group D |
| Fertilizer | Fertilizer/lime | Manure/fertilizer | Mulch |

Year 1

| Group A | Group B | Group C | Group D |
| Manure/fertilizer | Fertilizer | Fertilizer/lime | Mulch |

Manures, Fertilizers and Feeding

MANURES and fertilizers differ in composition and serve different purposes. Manures are derived from animal and vegetable remains and are bulky, with low concentrations of plant nutrients. They are normally dug in or given as a mulch in considerable quantity – 3 or more kg/m² (6½ lb/sq yd). Fertilizers consist of concentrated organic material of plant or animal origin, or of inorganic mineral matter, and are usually rich in plant nutrients. They are used before or after sowing or planting at rates of 35–140 g/m² (1–4 oz/sq yd).

Manures, as well as peat and compost improve and maintain soil fertility. The moisture and nutrient holding capacities of light sandy soils are increased. Heavy clay soils are rendered easier to cultivate and surplus water can drain away more readily. Fertilizers are necessary to replace nutrients taken up by crops, lost in drainage or temporarily absorbed by bacteria.

MANURES AND FERTILIZERS AVAILABLE

The normally obtainable bulky manures include farmyard manure, spent mushroom compost, peat and bark fibre. Fertilizers can be bought as balanced mixtures of nitrogen, phosphate and potash, and applied either as a slow-acting base dressing before sowing or planting, or as a quick-acting topdressing, liquid feed or foliar spray given to growing crops. These mixtures can be made up from fertilizers listed in the table opposite.

IS COMPOST EASY TO MAKE ?

Follow a few simple rules and compost making will present few problems. Use non-woody, vegetable material free of pests and diseases, including lawn mowings, leaves and household waste, but exclude troublesome weeds like couch grass, bellbine and convolvulus. Encourage rapid rot-down by using bins or heaps large enough to heat up, and ensure contents are not too acid. Compost in bins retains heat better than heaps and keeps out winter rains. Cover heaps with a layer of soil or plastic. Apply proprietary activator or nitrogenous fertilizer and lime. In three to six months compost will be ready to dig out from the bottom of the bin or heap.

WHEN LIME IS NEEDED

Vegetables differ in their requirements of lime in the soil. The cabbage family needs lime more than most to help combat Club Root disease. Potatoes and root vegetables need least. Evenly scatter ground limestone at 200 g/m² (6 oz/sq yd) before planting members of the cabbage family. Where crop rotation is practised, each strip will be systematically limed one year in three. Soils on chalk or limestone do not normally need lime but, if in doubt, a soil test kit should provide a reasonable guide.

Fertilizer	Content %	Origin	Type and Use
Bone Meal	4N 21P	Organic	Slow-acting. Pre-planting
Hoof and Horn	12–14N	Organic	Slow-acting. Pre-planting
Nitrate of Potash	15N 35K	Inorganic	Quick-acting. Post-planting
Nitro Chalk	16–20N	Inorganic	Quick-acting. Post-planting
Sulphate of Ammonia	21N	Inorganic	Moderate to quick-acting. Pre-/post-planting.
Sulphate of Potash	48–50K	Inorganic	Moderate to quick-acting. Pre-/post-planting
Superphosphate	16–18P	Inorganic	Moderate to quick-acting. Pre-/post-planting

Key.   N=Nitrogen   P=Phosphate   K=Potash   Pre-planting=base fertilizer   Post-planting=topdressing or liquid feed.

COMPOST BINS

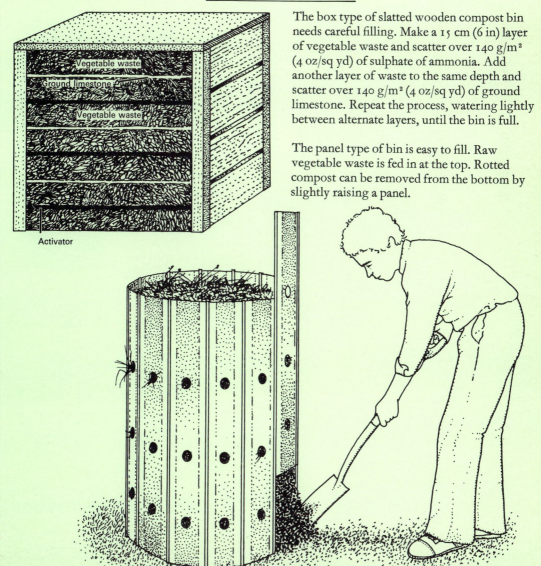

The box type of slatted wooden compost bin needs careful filling. Make a 15 cm (6 in) layer of vegetable waste and scatter over 140 g/m^2 (4 oz/sq yd) of sulphate of ammonia. Add another layer of waste to the same depth and scatter over 140 g/m^2 (4 oz/sq yd) of ground limestone. Repeat the process, watering lightly between alternate layers, until the bin is full.

The panel type of bin is easy to fill. Raw vegetable waste is fed in at the top. Rotted compost can be removed from the bottom by slightly raising a panel.

Tools and Equipment

Tools fall into two categories – the essential and the desirable. When starting from scratch, obtain a few essential items, such as a spade, garden fork, rake, dibber and trowel. Others can be added as need or experience decree.

Just like other commodities, there are many variations of even the most basic tool. Generally, they should be of well proven design and strongly constructed and of suitable size, weight and balance for the user. Tools are a long term investment, so non-rot and corrosion-proof materials are highly desirable. Stainless steel is ideal, although it is rather expensive.

Tools and equipment should be properly cared for and stored correctly. When not in use, they should be cleaned thoroughly, wiped over with an oily rag and stored neatly under cover. Sharp tools require less effort to use, do a better job and last longer than rusty, neglected ones.

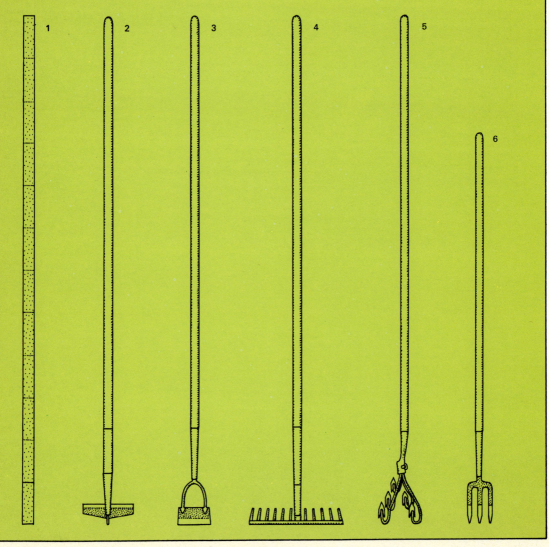

1 **Measuring stick** can be made from a strip of timber with saw notches for the scale

2 **Draw hoe,** useful for chopping down weeds on heavy soil and for earthing up

3 **Dutch hoe** cuts through weeds with a push/pull action, used on light soils

4 **Garden rake** is essential for working in fertilizer and in seedbed preparations

5 **Five pronged cultivator** is useful for breaking down ground in spring after autumn digging

6 **Long handled weed-fork**

7 **Digging or potato fork** is handy on stony soil or in wet sticky clay conditions

8 **Garden fork,** ideal for digging, working in manure and loosening compacted soil

9 **Garden spade treaded,** the most basic and essential of all tools for ground preparation

10 **Galvanized metal wheelbarrow**

11 **Hand or weed fork**

12 **Trowel for planting out**

13 **Garden reel and line** for straight rows

14 **Dibber** for planting out young plants

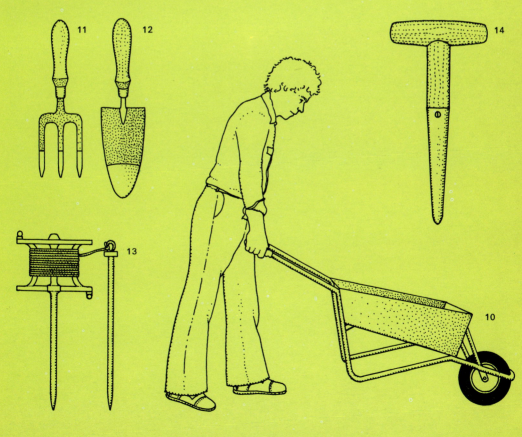

Sowing Seed

For successful cultivation, start by obtaining fresh seed from a reputable source. Bear in mind that good seed, although initially more expensive, costs no more to grow-on than poor seed, but the end results are likely to be more rewarding. Select varieties best suited to the time of year and purpose. Choose hardy varieties for cool districts and sites. Prepare the seedbed thoroughly and use clean composts and containers indoors. Sow seeds in good time to ensure proper growth and development, making succession sowings as required. Sow at the correct depth and spacing, using the methods best suited to individual crops. Supply the best possible conditions for germination, ensuring adequate warmth, moisture and protection from weeds, pests and diseases. After sowing outdoors, protect seedbeds from pets and birds. Indoors, cover containers with glass and then paper to conserve moisture and exclude light.

WHAT TO DO

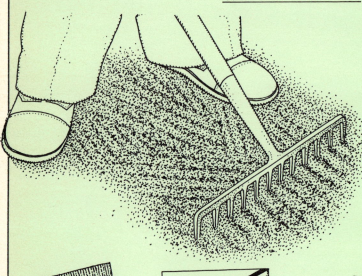

Seedbed Preparation
After digging or forking, firm the seedbed by treading heel-to-toe fashion. When conditions are right, especially on light or sandy land, the soil does not stick to the feet or to tools. Apply fertilizer 10–14 days before sowing and rake in to a depth of about 8 cm (3 in). Break down all lumps and work the soil to a fine tilth or crumb consistency, leaving a smooth surface.

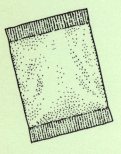

Seed Treatment
For good germination buy seeds which are foil wrapped, pelleted, or dusted with fungicide or pesticide. Soak hard coated seeds, like spinach and peas, before sowing.

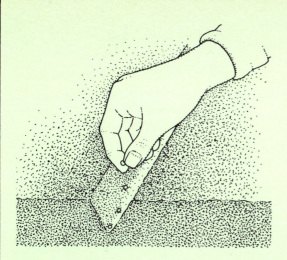

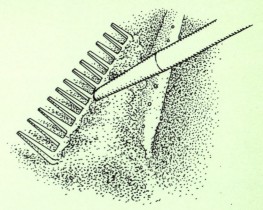

Seed Placement

A popular method is to sow seeds thinly, a pinch at a time between finger and thumb in shallow drills. Sow pelleted seeds individually at half the final spacing to allow for losses.

Covering Seed

Rake fine soil over the seeds and gently tamp the surface. Where soil is sticky, cover seeds with a sandy compost. Cover seeds which can be broadcast by sieving over fine soil.

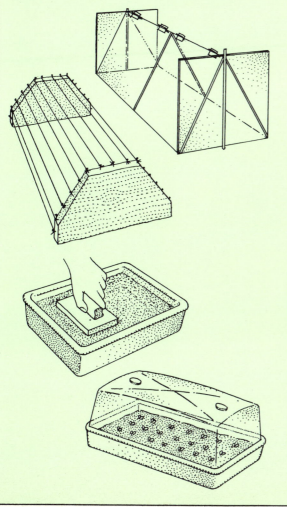

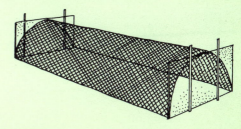

Protection

Early in the year, cover seed drills with cloches for extra warmth. Protect newly-sown seeds from birds with black cotton threads stretched above the soil or place wire guards over crops vulnerable to attacks by pigeons.

Container Sowing

Cover the bottom of each container with a shallow layer of fine gravel and fill to the rim with moist seed compost. Remove any surplus compost by drawing a piece of wood, saw-fashion, across the top of each container. Gently press a firmer – a flat piece of wood or metal – on to the compost, to leave a smooth level surface about 6 mm ($\frac{1}{4}$ in) below the rim. Water each container, using a watering can with fine rose, and allow to drain. Sow the seeds thinly on the surface and cover with fine compost. Place a sheet of glass on each container and cover with paper to exclude light. Germinate the seeds in warmth as necessary, keeping them moist.

Thinning and Transplanting

WHERE it is possible to sow seeds sufficiently far apart, it is neither necessary nor desirable to thin or transplant. With carrots, in particular, sowing thinly to begin with is preferable to thinning later, with the attendant dangers of attracting Carrot Fly. Thinning is necessary to avoid spindly, disease prone plants, which result from overcrowded, thickly sown seedlings. Selective removal of seedlings diminishes competition for space, light and moisture, the conditions favourable for improved growth and quality. Transplanting is useful in two ways. Firstly, it enables increased use to be made of small plots and, secondly, it helps to fill up gaps in rows of plants. When growing cauliflowers, for example, a small corner can accommodate many seedlings for 6–8 weeks, until they are ready for setting out. Thus, large areas of ground are occupied for shorter periods than if sown direct and thinned.

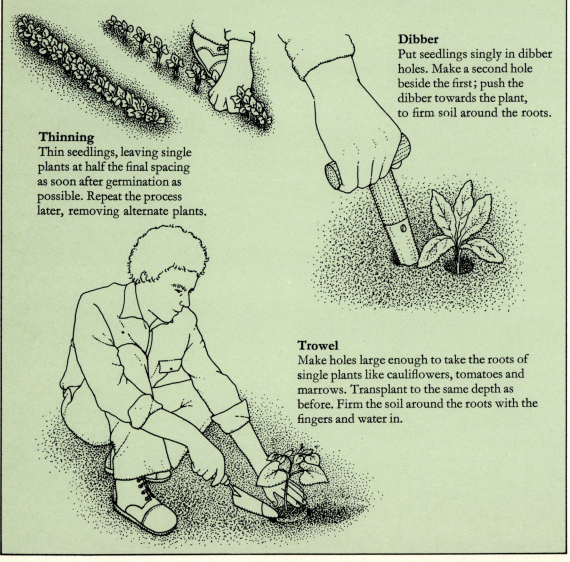

Dibber
Put seedlings singly in dibber holes. Make a second hole beside the first; push the dibber towards the plant, to firm soil around the roots.

Thinning
Thin seedlings, leaving single plants at half the final spacing as soon after germination as possible. Repeat the process later, removing alternate plants.

Trowel
Make holes large enough to take the roots of single plants like cauliflowers, tomatoes and marrows. Transplant to the same depth as before. Firm the soil around the roots with the fingers and water in.

Forms of Cover

THE protection of crops allows the maximum use of an area much larger than that actually covered; for example, in the raising of plants for setting out. Other benefits include the growing of out-of-season and tender crops. When buying, make sure full light is admitted and structures are well ventilated, of good design and sound construction. Aluminium alloy or other rot- and corrosion-proof material is preferable for trouble-free maintenance.

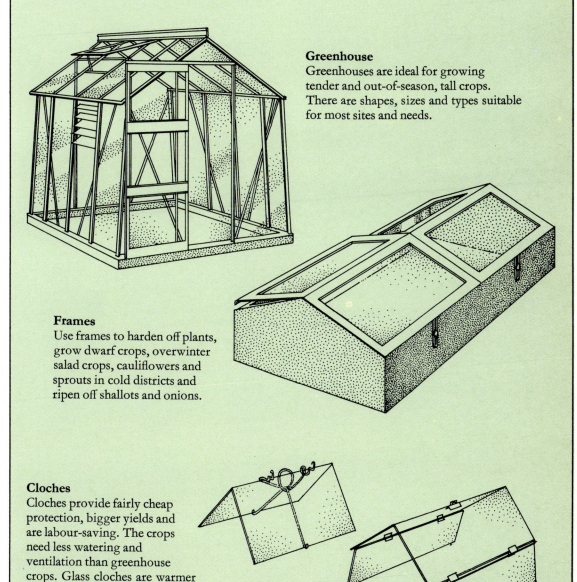

Greenhouse
Greenhouses are ideal for growing tender and out-of-season, tall crops. There are shapes, sizes and types suitable for most sites and needs.

Frames
Use frames to harden off plants, grow dwarf crops, overwinter salad crops, cauliflowers and sprouts in cold districts and ripen off shallots and onions.

Cloches
Cloches provide fairly cheap protection, bigger yields and are labour-saving. The crops need less watering and ventilation than greenhouse crops. Glass cloches are warmer in winter than plastic ones. Those over 30 cm (12 in) wide and 25 cm (10 in) high are most useful.

Globe Artichoke

THE globe artichoke can be grown without difficulty in well-drained land, if given protection from severe frost. It needs considerable space and so it is best suited to medium to large gardens. This vegetable is becoming increasingly popular but is usually considered more of a luxury than a staple. Globe artichokes make stately, handsome, silvery plants and, when left unharvested, produce large purple flowers on long stems.

Treat as perennial
Soil : light to medium, well manured loam
Site : sheltered and sunny
Plant : April and May
Varieties : Green Ball, Green Globe
Yield : six or more buds per plant

SOWING/PLANTING

Sow seed in March in containers at a minimum temperature of 16°C (61°F). Prick out singly into pots, harden off in frames ready for planting out in May. Remove suckers, rooted side growths, from parent plants in October and pot up singly. Overwinter in unheated frames and harden off for setting out in April/May. Rake in 100 g/m² (3 oz/sq yd) of balanced fertilizer. Set plants out 1·2 m (4 ft) apart each way on land available for four years. Set out seed raised plants 30 cm (12 in) apart in nursery beds. Plant in final positions next spring.

AFTERCARE

Keep plants well watered and weed-free. Place a triangle of 1·8 m (6 ft) canes around each plant. Loop string round plant and canes at 30 cm (12 in) intervals. In the following spring and in subsequent years, rake in 70 g/m² (2 oz/sq yd) of balanced fertilizer and then mulch. Where growth is slow, give an occasional liquid feed, from the tight bud stage until harvesting. Shorten the old stems to 20 cm (8in) after harvesting to produce edible shoots. Cut all stems to 15 cm (6 in) above ground in autumn. Discard old plants in the third/ fourth cropping season and replace.

HARVESTING

The buds are ripe when the outer scales begin to open but the central scales are still tightly folded. For established plants this will be in July and for those in their first year in August or September. Cut the buds with a short length of stem attached, choosing cool conditions. Vigorous two- and three-year-old plants produce new shoots or chards when cut back after harvesting. Blanch these 45 cm (18 in) shoots by wrapping in black plastic and earth up. Cut off blanched shoots at soil level about six weeks later.

SPECIAL POINTS

The bonus crop of succulent chards is well worth the extra work involved in blanching. Protect the crowns of plants from severe seasonal frosts by covering with a 10 cm (4 in) layer of straw or leaves which can be held in place with 2·5 cm (1 in) mesh wire netting pegged down.

Jerusalem Artichoke

THE Jerusalem artichoke is an easily grown vegetable, tolerant of a wide range of conditions, but a well-drained soil is essential. It grows to over 1·8 m (6 ft) in height. Very rich soils result in excessive top growth, so avoid heavy applications of fertilizers. However, moderate dressings of well-rotted manure or compost can result in heavier than average crops. Flowering reduces crop yield so remove the tip when buds are seen.

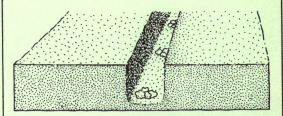

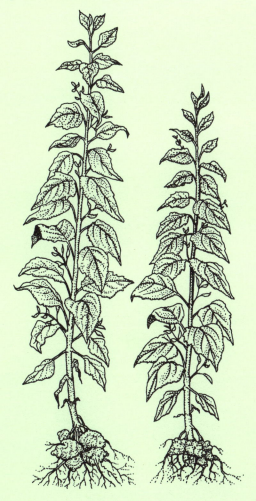

PLANTING
Lightly manure poor soils when digging. Rake in 70 g/m² (2 oz/sq yd) of balanced fertilizer 7–10 days before planting, except on deep, rich ground. Set the tubers out 10–15 cm (4–6 in) deep and 35 cm (14 in) apart in the rows, with 75 cm (2½ ft) between rows. Erect 1·8 m (6 ft) posts at the ends of rows where crop is used as screen.

AFTERCARE
Weed regularly. Mulch in May. Water in dry weather and feed in May and July with balanced fertilizer at a rate of 35 g/m² (1 oz/sq yd). Earth up in early August and again in autumn. Remove the growing point before flowering unless the plants are being used as a screen, when support between parallel wires is needed. Cut down top growth when the leaves wither.

HARVESTING
Leave tubers in the ground until required for use and protect with soil or straw. First cut down the foliage to 20 cm (8 in) then ease up the roots with a fork. Lift one root at a time, making sure no tubers are left behind. They do not store well, but, if it is necessary to lift before use, carefully remove any soil from sound tubers and store in moist peat in frost-free conditions.

Treat as an annual
Soil: light loam
Site: sunny or light shade
Plant: February to April
Varieties: New White – white skinned, Fuseau – purple skinned
Yield: 1·5–2·0 kg (3–4 lb) per plant

Asparagus

ASPARAGUS is a luxurious, early summer vegetable, ready for harvesting in April or May over a period of about six weeks. It is easy and inexpensive to grow in permanent beds. It occupies the land continuously for up to 20 years. Most soils suit this hardy crop, but free drainage is essential and the land must be clean and free of perennial weeds. Given reasonable attention, the size and quality of the shoots will improve each year.

60 cm (2 ft) apart in rows 60 cm (2 ft) apart and cover with 5–8 cm (2–3 in) fine soil. Do not leave the roots exposed. Plants can be grown from seed sown thinly in an outdoor seedbed in 3 cm (1 in) deep drills. Thin plants to 15 cm (6 in) apart. Plant out crowns the following year, but cropping will not begin for another 2–3 years.

AFTERCARE

Gradually fill up the trench in the first growing season by drawing soil over the roots. After harvesting, let the stems grow on and support if necessary. In summer pick the berries from female plants. When the foliage turns yellow in autumn cut off the stems 3 cm (1 in) above soil level and mulch the plants. In March, topdress with 100 g/m² (3 oz/sq yd) balanced fertilizer and gently work in. Hand weed the bed each spring.

Perennial
Soil: light to medium loam
Site: open and sunny
Sow/plant: April

SOWING/PLANTING

In autumn, double-dig and generously manure the bed. Lime acid soils. In spring, dig trenches 30 cm (12 in) deep and fork in 135 g/m² (4 oz/sq yd) of balanced fertilizer 10 days before planting. Set out crowns

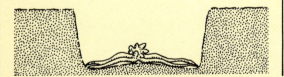

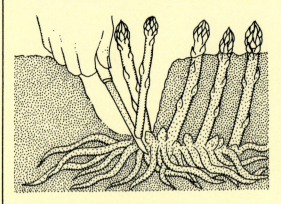

HARVESTING

Do not cut any shoots in the first season after planting; in the second, take only a few. Once the bed is established, cut harder over a longer period. With a sharp serrated knife, cut 10–15 cm (4–6 in) shoots well below soil level, avoiding other stems.

Harvest asparagus
when the spears are 10–15 cm
(4–6 in) long but stop cutting after
late June to avoid exhausting the crowns.

Pick broad beans when the pods are well filled.
Check that the seeds are tender and that the eyes have
not turned brown or black.

Broad Beans

Broad beans are relatively easy to grow. They are hardy and heavy yielding and can give a supply of vegetables from early June through August. The plants grow to 1 m (3 ft) or more, but there are dwarf varieties for small plots. Broad beans will grow on any well dug piece of land but they do not thrive in over wet or over acid conditions. When there is a glut any surplus can be frozen. The greenseeded varieties are especially suitable for freezing.

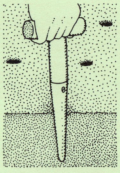

Seeds can be sown quickly and easily, using a dibber when conditions allow. Make 5 cm (2 in) deep holes, placing one seed in each and cover with soil.

Provide support for taller Longpod beans. Erect 1 m (3 ft) stakes on both sides of the row. Loop string from stake to stake.

Annual
Soil: any fertile, well-manured soil which is well drained
Site: open and sunny
Sow/plant: Sow November–April, plant March.

SOWING/PLANTING

In autumn or winter double-dig and manure the site. In spring, lime acid soils. Ten days later rake in 100 g/m² (3 oz/sq yd) balanced fertilizer. Sow the beans 7 cm (3 in) deep in double staggered rows 22 cm (9 in) apart. Allow 20 cm (8 in) between plants and 60–90 cm (2–3 ft) between the double rows. Cover with cloches or protect from birds. Broad beans may be sown in autumn on well-drained soils in warm areas.

AFTERCARE

Keep down the weeds by hoeing. Pinch out the growing point – the top 5–7 cm (2–3 in) of growth – as soon as the bottom pods have set. This helps to control Black Fly which often attacks the tips of the plant, and to divert nutrients to the developing beans.

HARVEST

Harvest beans 16–30 weeks after sowing. Take a few at a time from each plant when they are of good size but before they are mature and hard. After harvesting cut down the tops for compost and dig the nitrogen-rich roots into the soil.

Dwarf French Beans

THE French bean is a tender plant but, by protecting the earliest and latest crops with cloches and by making successive sowings either under glass or outdoors, it is possible to harvest from June through to mid-November. This is an easy to grow crop and doesn't normally require staking. These beans do best on well-drained land. Improve heavy soils by forking in plenty of manure or compost. Beans surplus to immediate requirements are ideal for freezing.

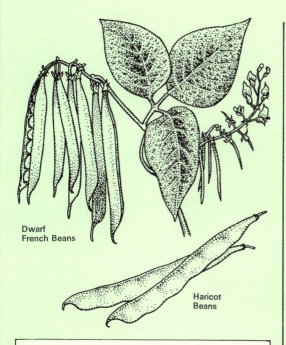

Dwarf French Beans

Haricot Beans

Annual
Soil: light, well-drained
Site: sheltered, sunny
Sow: mid-March to mid-July
Varieties: Green, Yellow and Purple podded, Haricot

SOWING/PLANTING

Double-dig and manure the site in the autumn. In spring, lime acid soils. A week later, rake in 100 g/m² (3 oz/sq yd) balanced fertilizer. Sow seeds 12 cm (5 in) apart in 5 cm (2 in) deep drills, 45 cm (18 in) apart. Plant out indoor-raised plants in June. Sow seven seeds to a 20 cm (8 in) pot in March. Grow on indoors or in a cold frame to give a crop in June. Support with sticks.

AFTERCARE

Hoe regularly and water in dry weather as necessary. Control slugs with bait. After a hot day, while the beans are setting, syringe the plants with water to assist fruit set. On exposed or wet sites, support plants with twiggy sticks. At the beginning of October, put cloches over late sowings to keep them cropping until November.

HARVESTING

Pick the pods when they are young and tender. If left on the plants too long, they become stringy and fewer new pods are formed. Haricots are harvested after the seeds have ripened. Cut down the tops after harvesting and dig in the roots.

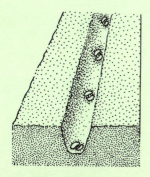

Runner Beans

ALTHOUGH runner beans are the most demanding of all the beans, they are heavy croppers and repay good cultivation. Avoid extremes of soil types, such as very heavy clays or light sands. Harvested from late July to October, runner beans are more flavoursome but coarser than French beans. They make a decorative screen with scarlet or white flowers. The tall varieties are most commonly grown but the dwarf kinds are well worth a try. Any surplus is ideal for freezing.

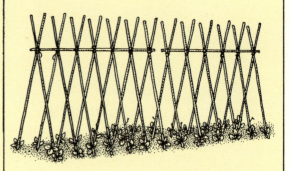

Train runners up pairs of 2·4 m (8 ft) poles set 45 cm (18 in) apart, crossed and tied together 15 cm (6 in) from the top. To secure, tie a pole horizontally along the top. Alternatively, they can be trained up wires round a central pole or to wire mesh fixed to poles at each end of the row.

Treat as annual
Soil: fertile, medium loam
Site: warm, sunny and sheltered
Sow: under cover April, outdoors May to June

SOWING/PLANTING

In late autumn double-dig and work in manure with the topsoil. In spring, lime acid soils. After a week rake in fertilizer 60 g/m (2 oz/3 ft) run of trench. Avoid excess which encourages growth at the expense of yield. Sow seeds singly 5 cm (2 in) deep and 30 cm (12 in) apart with 45 cm (18 in) between the double row. Harden off indoor-raised plants and plant out in June when they are 5–8 cm (2–3 in) high.

AFTERCARE

Cover seedlings sown in April with cloches until the danger of frost is past. Control slugs with bait. Plants can be stopped when 60 cm (2 ft) high and grown as a ground crop. Stop all plants when they reach the top of their supports. Syringe plants in the evenings in hot weather to assist flower set. Water the the plants well and a 3 cm (1 in) mulch helps to conserve moisture. As pods develop, feed the plants weekly with dilute liquid fertilizer.

HARVESTING

Pick young pods before seeds begin to swell. The harder they are picked the more pods will be formed. Hold stem with one hand and pull pods downwards with the other. After harvesting cut down plants and burn, digging in the nitrogen-rich roots.

Beetroot

BEETROOT is a simply grown, hardy, root vegetable requiring little space. It is relatively easy to maintain a year-round supply. Globe beet are tender and useful for salads from June onwards, whereas the Long-rooted and Intermediate types are ideal for growing to maturity and storing for use right through to April or May. Do not grow this crop on freshly manured land. For the production of tender roots it is essential to create conditions which maintain rapid growth.

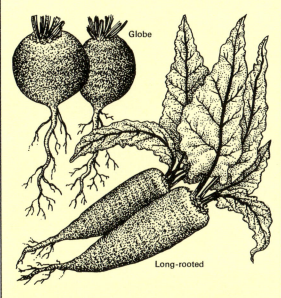

Globe

Long-rooted

Treat as an annual
Soil: well worked, fertile, light
Site: open, unshaded
Sow: March to June
Varieties: Globe, Intermediate- and Long-rooted

SOWING

Land, which has been manured for a previous crop, should be dug in autumn. Beet thrives on deeply worked, free-draining, light, sandy land. Prior to sowing, rake in 100 g/m² (3 oz/sq yd) of balanced fertilizer and work down to a fine tilth to create quick-growing conditions. Sow seeds thinly in 3 cm (1 in) deep drills 30 cm (1 ft) apart for Globe and 45 cm (18 in) for Long-rooted types. Sow earliest Globes in frames or cloches in March and Long-rooted maincrop in May.

AFTERCARE

Water seedlings in dry weather to encourage continued rapid growth. If growth is slow, give a feed of nitro-chalk at the rate of 20 g/m² (½ oz/sq yd). Thin to 5 cm (2 in) apart when the first three or four rough leaves appear. Thin finally 3–4 weeks later, removing alternate plants, to 10–12 cm (4–5 in) apart; the thinnings of Globe beet can be used in salads. Hoe regularly but do not touch the beet or they will bleed.

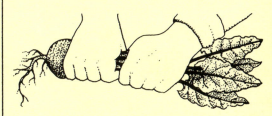

HARVESTING

Harvest Globe beet from June onwards when they are no bigger than tennis balls. Water the ground 12 hours before lifting which can then be readily carried out. Remove the leaves with 4 cm (1½ in) of stalk remaining by twisting not cutting in order to prevent bleeding and loss of colour. If allowed to grow on, they will become hard and woody. Lift maincrop Long- and Intermediate-rooted kinds in October. Lift the roots carefully using a fork, as any damaged roots will bleed. Store in a cool, frost-free place indoors, placing the beet in layers in boxes of peat or sand. In milder districts the roots can be left in the ground until required, provided they are covered with straw to protect from severe frosts.

Sprouting Broccoli

THESE hardy vegetables provide succulent spears between autumn and spring. The green varieties are the least hardy and are usually harvested in autumn. Late purple and white types occupy the ground for about 12 months and produce curdlike clusters of light purple and white buds respectively. Perennial broccoli plants produce 6–8 small curds every year, if regularly mulched and fed. All types of broccoli can be frozen when surplus to requirements.

Insert plants in dibber holes up to the lowest leaves, 60 cm (2 ft) apart each way. Lever soil firmly around the roots using the dibber. Plant green sprouting broccoli first.

AFTERCARE

Hoe regularly and water after planting and during dry spells. Protect against slugs and pigeons. In summer, spray with derris or fenitrothion if the crop is attacked by caterpillars. Hoe in 35 g/m² (1 oz/sq yd) of nitro-chalk about six weeks after planting. For green sprouting varieties repeat this 4 weeks later. With other types of broccoli repeat early next March.

Biennial or perennial
Soil: fertile, deep, well-drained loam
Site: sheltered, sunny
Sow: April–May for planting May–June
Varieties: green, purple and white
Yield: 0·5 kg (1 lb) per plant

HARVESTING

First cut the curd of green varieties then gather the side growths. Harvest purple and white kinds when the spears are 10 cm (4 in) long – cut hard to prevent flowering. Freeze any surplus.

SOWING/PLANTING

Sow seeds thinly 1 cm ($\frac{1}{2}$ in) deep in moist drills on a well-prepared, limed seedbed. Keep well watered. Dust seedlings with derris against Flea Beetle. Before planting, dig and work in manure on light soils. Later, lime and leave the land to settle. Rake in 100 g/m² (3 oz/sq yd) of base fertilizer 10 days before planting. Soak the seedbed 24 hours before lifting the young plants with a fork. Dust the dibber holes with bromophos and calomel against Root Fly and Club Root.

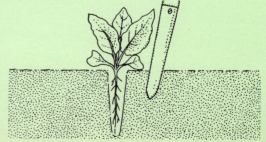

Brussels Sprouts

BRUSSELS sprouts are a popular, hardy vegetable. They require a long season of growth, about 8 months, to develop to the full. The plants are raised in seedbeds and transplanted for cropping. By using a succession of early and late varieties, it is possible to maintain a supply from August to February. Each plant has a fairly long harvesting period. To guard against Club Root avoid acid land and sites where cabbage cropped the previous year.

Treat as a hardy biennial
Soil: non-acid, rich and firm
Site: unshaded, open
Sow: February under glass to April outdoors
Varieties: early and late

SOWING/PLANTING

Sow early varieties in warmth in February. Prick out, harden off and plant out in April to May under cloches. Sow maincrop mid-March under cloches and late varieties in the open in mid-April. Sow thinly in drills 1 cm ($\frac{1}{2}$ in) deep in a prepared seedbed. This crop needs a firm bed. Dig deeply in autumn and manure well. Lime acid land in spring and a week later apply 100 g/m² (3 oz/sq yd) of balanced fertilizer. Rake in and level before planting out seedlings 10–15 cm (4–6 in) high. Plant firmly as deep as the first seed leaves. Space plants 68 cm (2 ft 3 in) apart both ways. Water well until established.

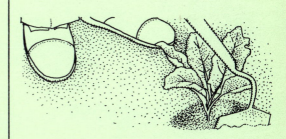

AFTERCARE

Hoe regularly. Water in dry weather. Earth up the plants as winter approaches to make them firm. When the lowest leaves turn yellow, break them off. Protect plants from birds and animals. Spray against caterpillars and aphids, if these are troublesome.

HARVESTING

As they mature, pick sprouts from the bottom with a downward tug, leaving the smaller buttons to develop. After harvesting these, use the cabbage-like top as a vegetable. Surplus sprouts can be frozen.

Cabbage

THE least demanding of the brassicas, this is an easy crop to grow. With forward planning cabbage can be harvested all the year round, using a succession of different types and varieties. Quick growing summer varieties, slower autumn and winter varieties including savoys and spring cabbage form the three main groups which differ in texture and flavour. The general practice is to sow in seedbeds and transplant, but some are grown *in situ*.

Spring cabbage

Autumn cabbage

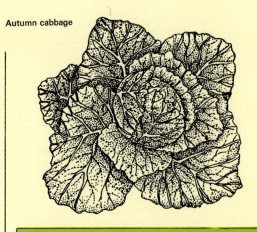

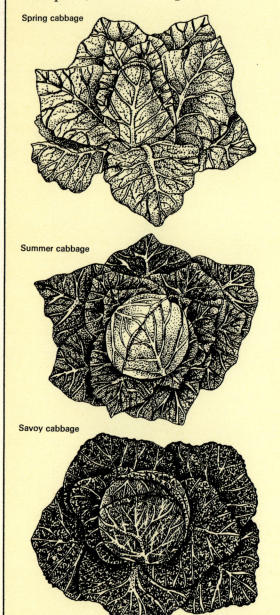

Summer cabbage

Savoy cabbage

Treat as annual
Soil: any good garden soil
Site: sheltered and sunny
Sow: For summer and autumn cutting: January–February in warmth, March–April in frames or cloches, April–May outdoors
Outdoors: April–June for winter use, early August for spring use
Varieties: pointed and roundheaded

SOWING/PLANTING

Make earliest sowings in warmth and germinate at 7°C (45°F). Prick out seedlings 4 cm (1½ in) apart in No 2 potting compost. Harden off and plant out 8–10 weeks after sowing. Outdoors, prepare firm seedbeds on fresh ground by digging, forking and liming, except on chalk soils. Rake down to a fine tilth. Where crops are to be sown *in situ* and thinned, first rake in 100 g/m² (3 oz/sq yd) of balanced fertilizer. Sow thinly 1 cm (½ in) deep in moist drills, covering the seed with fine soil, which can be scuffled over with your feet.

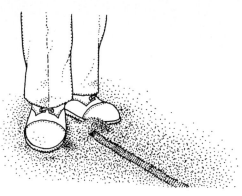

Collards, grown for cutting young from November, are sown thinly in July *in situ* and thinned to 10–12 cm (4–5 in). Varieties like Hispi F1 hybrid are treated similarly.

Prepare land manured for a previous crop by digging, liming, raking and applying fertilizer, as above. Set out plants. Dust the holes made by the trowel or dibber with bromophos and calomel to check Root Fly and Club Root. Space summer, autumn and winter varieties 60 cm (2 ft) apart each way. Set autumn-planted spring cabbage 30 cm (12 in) apart with 45 cm (18 in) between rows.

AFTERCARE

Water in plants immediately after setting out. Hoe regularly and keep moist. Protect against slugs and birds. Thin out direct sown crops to 30 cm (12 in). Those used as collards or spring greens may be grown closer together. Hoe in 35 g/m² (1 oz/sq yd) of nitro-chalk about a month after planting or thinning summer, autumn and winter varieties. For spring cabbage, wait until early March.

HARVESTING

In summer and autumn cut when sizeable heads have developed. Winter varieties can be left standing longer but only Savoys withstand severe weather. Burn old stumps as they do not rot down easily and can carry disease.

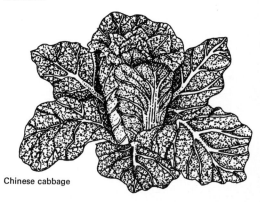

Chinese cabbage

SPECIAL POINTS

Chinese Cabbage
Quick-growing crop, maturing in three months. Sow seeds *in situ* in June, rows 40 cm (15 in) apart and thin to 30 cm (12 in). Some varieties will transplant but not all.

Savoy
Wrinkled leaved type. Easy to grow, maturing September onwards. Very hardy, stands well and valuable for late crops.

Spring Cabbage
Sow in August, plant out September and use the following April to June. If closely planted, thinnings can be used before.

Red Cabbage
Sow in spring, harvest in summer. Used chiefly for pickling.

Portuguese Cabbage
A connoisseur's vegetable of fine flavour. It is expensive to buy, but easy to grow. Sow in April, transplant in June and use in September to October.

Autumn/Winter Cabbage
Sow successively through April and May, plant out in June and pick from October.

Summer Cabbage
Sow in February to March, not too early or it runs to seed. Plant firm. Use June to October.

Carrots

Carrots are valuable for their high vitamin content. By making successive sowings of early and late types and using frames and cloches, young carrots can be harvested from June until the following spring. The maincrop stores well for winter use. There are three groups: short-rooted, useful for early forcing under cover and where land is rough or heavy; intermediate, slower growing but larger, sown in April for maincrop; and long-rooted as late maincrop.

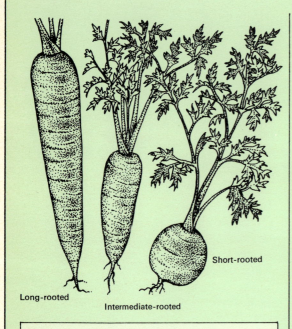

Long-rooted

Intermediate-rooted

Short-rooted

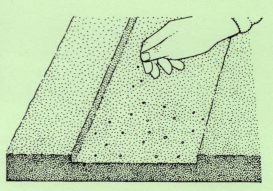

Treat as annual
Soil: rich, deep, light loam
Sites: full sun for earlies, maincrop tolerates partial shade
Sow: February and October to January under frames. April to July maincrop
Varieties: short-, intermediate- and long-rooted

SOWING

Dig land deeply in autumn and leave rough in the winter. Do not manure but use land manured for a previous crop. Before sowing, rake in 140 g/m² (4 oz/sq yd) fertilizer plus bromophos to control Carrot Fly. Work soil down as fine as possible as lumps or stones cause forking. Sow earlies in February to April, the first in a cold frame and, in March, on land warmed up under cloches, in July

and, in south, under frames from October to January. Sow maincrop types from April to mid-July. Sow thinly to reduce thinning (mixing with sand helps) in 1 cm ($\frac{1}{2}$ in) deep drills 30 cm (12 in) apart. Or broadcast seeds thinly over a bed or sow several rows about 7 cm (3 in) apart.

AFTERCARE

Thin earlies to 7 cm (3 in) and maincrop to 12 cm (5 in) in cool conditions when the soil is moist – less smell to attract the Carrot Fly. Firm soil round the remaining roots and water well. Remove thinnings immediately. Hoe regularly and water during dry weather to prevent roots splitting.

HARVESTING

Pull early carrots when large enough to use. Lift carrots for storing in early October. Later they become woody and crack. Lift with a fork. Use any damaged roots immediately to prevent Soft Rot attack in store. Cut off the leaves to within 1 cm ($\frac{1}{2}$ in) of the crown, remove any soil and store in boxes or heaps in layers with sand in a dry, well ventilated, frost-free shed.

Cauliflower

CAULIFLOWERS are the most difficult to grow and temperamental of all the cabbage family. They must be grown quickly and will not tolerate any form of setback. If, for example, seedlings are not hardened off sufficiently or if plants are allowed to dry out at any stage, the curds can be useless. With a careful choice of variety and attention to detail, it is possible to cut curds from May through to December. This crop is sown in a seedbed and transplanted.

Treat as an annual
Soil: deep, well-drained, medium loam
Site: sheltered, sunny
Sow: indoors in January, transplanted March–April; outdoors in April–May, transplanted June–July

SOWING/PLANTING

Sow in January in a heated greenhouse and in March in a cold frame for planting out in March to May. Sow outdoors in April or May for transplanting in June and July. Sow the seeds thinly in prepared and limed seedbeds in watered drills 1 cm ½ (in) deep and 15 cm (6 in) apart. To prepare the land for planting, double-dig and manure in the autumn. Lime in spring and allow to settle. Before planting, rake in 100 g/m² (3 oz/sq yd) fertilizer. Plant out when seedlings have 4–6 leaves. Water the seedbed the night before and lift carefully, using a fork. Discard any plants without a growing point. Use a dibber and treat holes with calomel against Club Root. Space plants 60 cm (2 ft) apart both ways. Plant firmly up to the lowest seed leaves. Water in after planting.

AFTERCARE

Hoe regularly and water in dry spells. An occasional liquid feed encourages rapid growth. Bend two leaves over the curds to protect against the weather. Control slugs and caterpillars and protect from birds.

HARVEST

Cut earliest heads from each batch when still small. This prolongs the duration of harvest. Freeze any surplus.

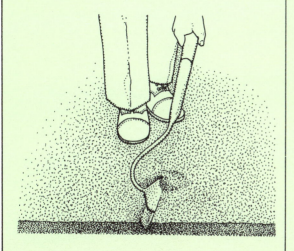

Celery

Two types of celery are commonly grown. Trench celery is hardy and needs earthing up to blanch; self-blanching is less hardy, milder flavoured and requires no earthing up but some protection. Celery is grown for its crisp stalks. It is easy to maintain a supply from mid-September through to March. Self-blanching celery is inclined to bolt, so aim to grow without check and do not plant too early. Plants are raised in warmth or bought in.

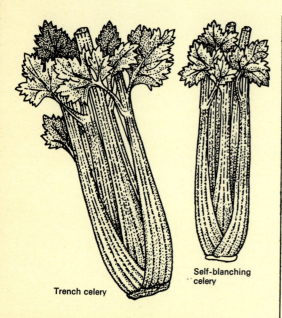

Trench celery

Self-blanching celery

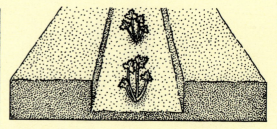

blanching celery, dig and manure the bed, work in 70 g/m² (2 oz/sq yd) of fertilizer. Set plants in blocks 22 cm (9 in) each way.

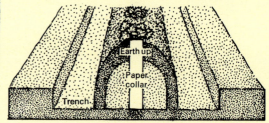

Earth up

Paper collar

Trench

Biennial
Soil: fertile, well-drained, moisture retentive
Site: open and sunny
Sow: April for planting out May/June

SOWING/PLANTING

Sow thinly in April on well moistened compost at about 16°C (61°F). When seedlings are 5 cm (2 in) prick out, grow on and harden off. In autumn or spring prepare trenches 30 cm (12 in) deep and 45 cm (18 in) wide. Fork up the bases, apply 15 cm (6 in) of manure, cover with 10 cm (4 in) of soil and leave to settle. Before planting, apply 70 g/m (2 oz/yd) of fertilizer. With a trowel, set the plants 22 cm (9 in) apart up the centre. Firm the roots and water in. For self-

AFTERCARE

Remove basal growths as they appear. Earth up trench celery when 35 cm (14 in) high in mid-August, with dry soil. Tie stems loosely then draw soil from the ridge half way up the stems. Three weeks later, draw it up to base of leaves. Earth up again after three weeks. Keep soil firm and off the leaves. Water generously and feed with liquid fertilizer throughout the summer. Remove any leaves with brown blisters and spray with malathion against Celery Fly.

HARVESTING

Self-blanching is ready from late August. Use before the onset of frost. Trench is ready 8 weeks after the first earthing. Open the ridge at one end, fork out crown. Close the ridge to protect from frost.

Varieties of outdoor ridge
cucumber, such as Baton
Vert, can produce heavy
crops of high quality. Pick
regularly to prolong fruiting.

Grow self-blanching celery
in blocks of several rows in level beds so
that the outer plants shade the stems of the inner ones.

Greenhouse and Frame Cucumbers

THIS crop demands attention to detail in cleanliness, in preparation of the growing bed, in training and in feeding. Cucumbers need plenty of warmth to start and are grown on under cover. The earliest cucumbers are edible in May; those grown cold about July. They must be grown quickly and without check for the best results. It is a climbing crop needing supports. Depending upon variety, fruits vary in size from 15–30 cm (6–12 in) long.

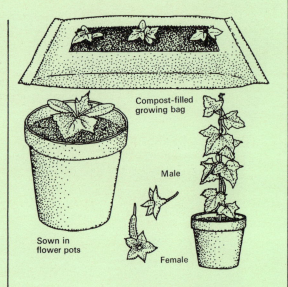

Compost-filled growing bag

Male

Sown in flower pots

Female

Annual
Soil: rich compost or bed
Site: under cover
Sow: February to May in warmth
Varieties: Greenhouse/Frame; and F1 Hybrids (all female)

SOWING

Sow seeds singly and on their edges in 7 cm (3 in) pots. Alternatively, sow them 3 cm (1 in) apart in boxes of seed compost. Cover with glass and a sheet of paper and place in a propagator at 24°C (75°F) or in the warmest part of the greenhouse, with a minimum night temperature of 18°C (64°F). Hybrids need warmer temperatures generally, with a minimum night temperature of 21°C (70°F). When the seeds germinate in 4–5 days, give maximum light and grow on at 16°C (61°F) for a month. Pot on the earliest plants singly into 12 cm (5 in) pots.

AFTERCARE

Two weeks before planting out, cover a hot bed with 7 cm (3 in) of peat-rich compost and soak. Set out plants deeply into bed or growing bag; the earliest in warmth. Tie to canes or vertical wires. Stop when the top is reached to encourage laterals. Train these on horizontal wires; stop at second leaf joint. Remove tendrils and male flowers. Grow two females (flowers, with small fruits behind) on each lateral. Syringe, water and keep humid. As fruits start to swell, liquid feed every 10 days. Mulch with equal parts soil and manure whenever root fibres appear. Shade from May to September. Protect from slugs and White Fly. In frames, stop the plants after the third leaf. Train laterals to fill up frame, stopping after 4–5 leaves. Grow one fruit per lateral.

HARVESTING

Well grown fruits are ready in 12–14 weeks.

Ridge Cucumbers

RIDGE cucumbers are reasonably hardy and are grown successfully outdoors in summer in a sunny, sheltered position. Excellent results can be obtained especially on light, well-drained soils. There is a wide variation in shapes and sizes, including gherkins. The bulk of the crop is harvested in August and September as the plants are killed by the onset of frosts. In cooler areas, it is, however, necessary to cover this crop with cloches.

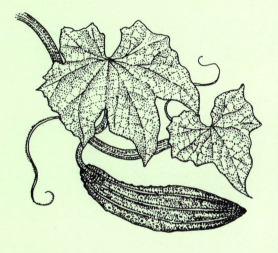

Soil :	deep, rich and well-drained
Site :	sheltered and in full sun
Sow :	April under cover; May outdoors
Varieties :	conventional and Japanese

AFTERCARE
Thin the direct sown plants when they have formed 2–4 leaves, removing the weaker plant from each spacing. Water afterwards. As soon as cucumbers have grown to 6 leaves, remove the growing point to

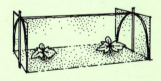

SOWING/PLANTING
Double-dig the land in autumn. In spring, dig out a 30 cm (12 in) trench. Fork a 15 cm (6 in) layer of well-rotted manure or compost into the bottom, cover with soil to form a ridge. Work in 100 g/m² (3 oz/sq yd) balanced fertilizer. Sow the earliest seeds, edgeways, in a cold greenhouse or frame in late April, 1 cm ($\frac{1}{2}$ in) deep in 7 cm (3 in) pots of seed compost. Harden off and plant out in June when frosts are over. With a trowel, set out 60 cm (2 ft) apart along the ridge. In warm districts, at the end of May, sow two seeds every 60 cm (2 ft) along the ridge and cover with cloches until established. Alternatively, sow seeds at 22 cm (9 in) and train plants up wire netting.

encourage bushy growth, aiming for 3–4 good side shoots. Do not remove the male flowers as the female flowers need to be fertilized in order to set fruit. To assist this, syringe regularly with clean water. Keep plants well-watered using a fine rose, but do not wash the soil away from the fibrous surface roots. When the cucumbers start to swell, liquid feed every 7 days. Protect all young growths from slugs and spray against Black Fly, if necessary.

HARVESTING
Cut the fruits when young to encourage continued fruit formation. When left, the plants tend to run to seed and cease cropping.

Popular Herbs

Herbs for culinary use are a garden bonus. They can be grown in odd corners but a herb plot is an absorbing hobby. They thrive in sunny, well-drained conditions and will grow in outdoor window boxes or pots. Individual herbs are grown for flowers, leaves or seeds. Drying is a popular way to preserve them. Strip large leaved types and lay on muslin; bundle small leaved kinds together and wrap in muslin before hanging to dry in a dark, airy room at 21°C (70°F).

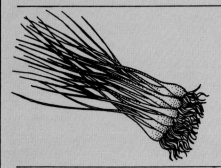

CHIVES
Position: average, well-drained soils in sun or shade.
Starting: sow seeds in early summer and thin to 30 cm (12 in). Split clumps of established plants every 3 years.
Harvesting: cut leaves close to the ground as required. Freeze for winter use or pot up clumps and grow on indoor windowsill. Loses colour when dried.
Note: an easy to grow, perennial herb. Mulch in spring and remove flowers as they appear.

PARSLEY
Position: fertile, deep, moist soil, a sheltered south-facing border is needed for winter cropping.
Starting: sow in March and July for year round use. Thin to 20 cm (8 in) apart.
Harvesting: cut as required. Deep freeze or dry.
Note: easy to grow but seeds are slow to germinate. Cover with cloches in September for winter use.

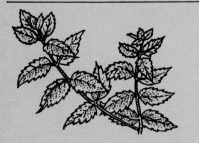

MINT
Position: rich, moist soil, partial shade or full sun.
Starting: lay 10 cm (4 in) pieces of root 15 cm (6 in) apart and 5 cm (2 in) deep in prepared beds. Established plants can be divided in autumn or spring.
Harvesting: cut as required. Dry or freeze for winter use or lift roots in September, plant in boxes of compost and grow indoors at 10°C (50°F) minimum.

SAGE
Position: average soil, but a warm site is needed to develop full flavour and aroma.
Starting: sow in May, transplant to nursery bed, and plant in final positions in autumn 40 cm (15 in) apart. Take soft wood cuttings in June. Sage is short-lived, so propagate new stock every third year.
Harvesting: pick leaves as required for use. Sage dries well, but cut shoots before flowering in May.

Herbs are a worthwhile addition to any
garden needing little space and a minimum of
care and attention.

BASIL
Position: choose the sunniest, warmest and most sheltered spot in the garden. In winter, grow indoors as a pot plant. Requires a light, rich soil.
Starting: sow annually in warmth in February at 13°C (55°F). Prick out and harden off. Plant out in June 30 cm (12 in) apart in prepared bed. It can be sown in growing bed in moist drills 1 cm (½ in) deep in May.
Harvesting: for immediate use, cut before the flowers open in August. Cut a second crop before frosts. Dry or freeze for winter.
Note: gives a spicy flavour to almost any dish.

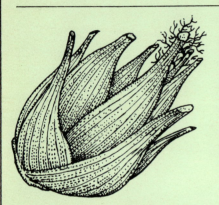

FENNEL
Position: full sun, average, well-drained soil.
Starting: sow seeds in April, 6 mm (¼ in) deep, in groups of 3, 45 cm (18 in) apart. Thin to leave the strongest. As plants deteriorate, sow every two years.
Harvesting: pick leaves as required. For seeds, cut stems in September, hang upside down in warm place, catch seeds and dry thoroughly before storing. Lift clumps of fresh fennel into peat; keep at 13°C (55°F) under cover in winter. Dry at 38°C (100°F). Pick in June for freezing. If seeds are not needed remove flowers.

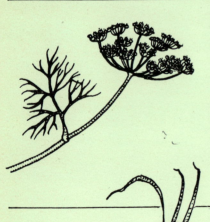

DILL
Position: well-drained but moist, fertile soil. Sunny.
Starting: sow annually in March–April in 6 mm (¼ in) deep, moist drills 23 cm (9 in) apart. Thin seedlings to 23 cm (9 in). Dill seeds itself readily and the resulting plants are often stronger than hand sown ones.
Harvesting: usually ready 6–8 weeks after sowing. Pick the young leaves as required. Cut stems in dry weather as seeds ripen in mid-August. Leaves are difficult to dry. Dry very slowly at below 38°C (100°F).
Note: both the leaves and seeds are used.

GARLIC
Position: full sun. Light, moist soil that has been well dug and manured in winter and allowed to settle.
Starting: in late February, work the soil down to a fine tilth and plant separated cloves 4 cm (1½ in) deep and 15 cm (6 in) apart with 30 cm (12 in) between rows. To give an early crop in June, plant cloves in October.
Harvesting: lift the bulbs when the leaves die down in July–August. Dry in sun. Hang up bulbs in dry cool conditions for storage.
Note: potent member of the onion family to be used with discretion. Pinch out the flower heads as soon as possible.

SWEET MARJORAM

Position: a well-drained, fertile soil in full sun is ideal for growing this herb.

Starting: sow annually from March to April under glass at 10–13 °C (50–55 °F). Harden off and plant out in May–June 30 cm (12 in) apart. Or sow in the open on well prepared land in May and thin to 30 cm (12 in).

Harvesting: pick leaves as required. For drying, pick just before the flowers open in June. Excellent, when combined with dried petals, for pot-pourri.

Note: the spicy flavoured leaves are good in meat and fish dishes and salads.

WINTER SAVORY

Position: sunny with well-drained, light soil.

Starting: sow seeds in late spring in 6 mm ($\frac{1}{4}$ in) deep drills. Thin to 30 cm (12 in) apart. Established plants can be divided in March–April. Take soft wood cuttings in May. Replace plants every 2–3 years.

Harvesting: use leaves as required. It is easy to dry, but this is not usually necessary as this herb is evergreen. The leaves are at their best just before flowering in July.

Note: this perennial evergreen with a sage-like taste is excellent in stews and salads.

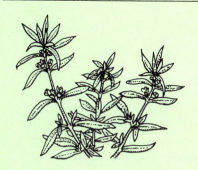

ROSEMARY

Position: in a sheltered, sunny border with well-drained, light soil.

Starting: sow in early spring. Thin as necessary and transplant to 60 cm (2 ft) apart. Can be sown in early summer in final position and thinned. Semi-hardwood cuttings can be taken in August or hardwood cuttings from September to March.

Harvesting: cut sprigs as required. Drying is satisfactory but not usually necessary.

Note: a highly aromatic evergreen shrub. Use sparingly.

THYME

Position: sunny on warm, average to light soils.

Starting: sow in growing bed in late spring. Thin, allowing 30 cm (12 in) between plants. Cuttings can be taken or plants divided in April or May.

Harvesting: for drying or freezing, cut just before the flowers open in June. However, it should not be necessary to dry this evergreen.

Note: this perennial evergreen flavours stuffings, soups and meat dishes. Combined with bay leaves and parsley, it is used in bouquets garnis. Beds should be remade every 3–4 years.

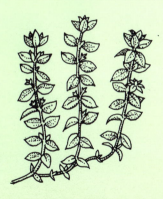

Lamb's Lettuce or Corn Salad

LAMB'S lettuce, sometimes known as corn salad, is a hardy annual continental salad plant. The leaves are crisp and tender and used in winter and spring salads, when few other salad vegetables are available. Since it grows in autumn and winter, the site is all important; it requires a sunny, sheltered, warm position. Lamb's lettuce can also be grown in pots of No 2 compost. This method is particularly good, as it keeps the low growing leaves clean.

Annual
Soil: well-drained, average soil
Site: sunny, sheltered, warm position
Sow: July–September and March–April

SOWING

Land which has been well-manured the previous winter for a summer vegetable crop is ideal for Lamb's lettuce. Rake down and apply 100 g/m² (3 oz/sq yd) of balanced fertilizer. Sow the seeds very thinly in 1 cm ($\frac{1}{2}$ in) deep, moist drills, spaced 15 cm (6 in) apart. Alternatively, broadcast the seeds thinly on a well prepared, fine bed. Make succession sowings every 14 days from the end of July to end September for a regular supply of fresh salad vegetables throughout the winter. Also an early sowing can be made in spring from March to April.

AFTERCARE

Thin the seedlings if necessary to 8–10 cm (3–4 in) apart. However, this should not, in fact, be necessary if the seeds were sown correctly and thinly in the first place. Control slugs with slug bait. Keep the soil off the low growing leaves. Do not allow the plants to flower. Protect from frost with straw or similar material, especially in early autumn when sudden, unexpected night frosts can severely damage or kill tender, young plants.

HARVESTING

When the plants have grown to approximately 15 cm (6 in) and developed 3–4 leaves, pull the plants up completely by the roots. Handle the plants carefully and take care not to damage the tender leaves. Cut off the roots, using a sharp knife, and use the leaves immediately.

SPECIAL POINTS

Use seed of cultivated varieties.
Grow plants quickly on fertile soil.
Protect from frost with cloches and ideally blanch the leaves as follows before gathering. Cover a few well grown plants at a time with inverted pots or boxes, two to three weeks before required to provide complete darkness. Cut or pick the leaves when pale green or creamy white.

Leeks

THIS extremely hardy crop is a valuable winter vegetable, especially in cold areas. Easy to grow and not as demanding as onions, it is comparatively trouble-free. It is sown in warmth under glass, under frames or cloches or in a seedbed outdoors, and then transplanted. It likes a long growing season and does well on land which has been manured and limed well in advance of planting. However, a very high standard of cultivation is needed to grow exhibition leeks.

Soil: free-draining, fertile but plenty of moisture
Site: open, sunny spot, sheltered from freezing winds
Sow: January under cover; March–April outdoors

SOWING/PLANTING
Sow under glass at the end of January, either with or without heat, spacing seeds 3 cm (1 in) apart in seed compost. Sift more compost over and firm gently. Harden off and plant out in April. Or, sow on a well-prepared seed bed under frames or cloches or in the open in March to April in moist drills 30–38 cm (12–15 in) apart. Thin seedlings to 4 cm (1½ in) apart. Transplant in June or July, when 15 cm (6 in) high. Water the seedbed 12 hours before. To prepare the growing bed, rake down to a fine tilth. Rake in 100 g/m² (3 oz/sq yd) balanced fertilizer. Make shallow trenches 38 cm (15 in) apart. Trim the top quarter of the leaves off the leek plants. Making dibber holes 15–23 cm (6–9 in) apart along the bottom of the trench, drop in plants as deep as the base of the leaves. Water in but do not firm.

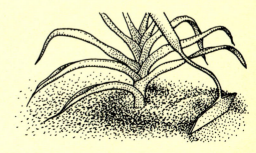

AFTERCARE
When the dibber holes have been filled up by rain or by watering, start to earth up gradually to blanch the leeks. Gently draw soil up to the leeks over a period of weeks – too quickly can lead to rotting. Hoe regularly and water in dry weather.

HARVESTING
Harvest crops sown in January, in August and those sown in April, from October to May. Leave the leeks in the ground until required for use and then ease out with a fork. Leeks stand well over winter.

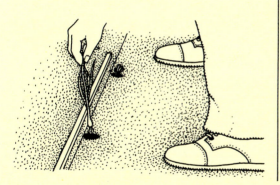

Lettuce

Wɪᴛʜ planning, careful choice of variety and cloches or a cold frame, lettuces can be grown all year. They need to be grown quickly without checks to growth or they run to seed. Once watering has begun, continue until the rains come or, again, they may run to seed. They make a useful catch crop. Of the two main types, cabbage is earlier maturing, while cos is better able to withstand drought, is of a fine flavour, but requires a longer growing season.

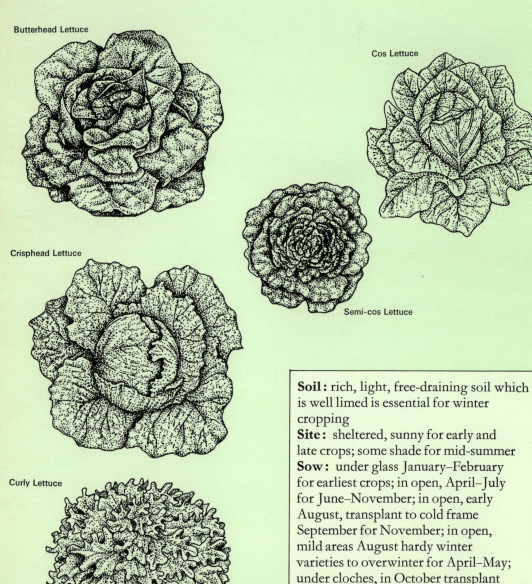

Butterhead Lettuce

Cos Lettuce

Crisphead Lettuce

Semi-cos Lettuce

Curly Lettuce

Soil: rich, light, free-draining soil which is well limed is essential for winter cropping
Site: sheltered, sunny for early and late crops; some shade for mid-summer
Sow: under glass January–February for earliest crops; in open, April–July for June–November; in open, early August, transplant to cold frame September for November; in open, mild areas August hardy winter varieties to overwinter for April–May; under cloches, in October transplant to frames December for April
Varieties: Butterheads, Crispheads, Cos types and Curly

SOWING/PLANTING

Dig ground and leave rough until planting time – autumn dig and manure land for summer crops. Lime soil, if acid. Before sowing or planting, work down to a fine tilth and apply 100 g/m² (3 oz/sq yd) balanced fertilizer. Sow seeds 1 cm (½ in) deep in drills spaced 30 cm (12 in) apart. Water drills before sowing and cover the seeds with fine soil, firming gently. Early in the year, make sowings in containers of seed compost, either in warmth or in a cold frame.

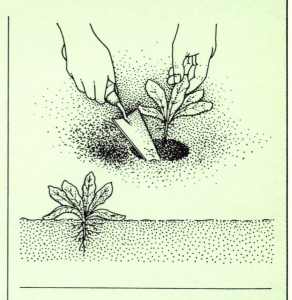

AFTERCARE

Control slugs with bait throughout the growing season and protect from birds. Keep well watered, avoiding dryness at the roots. Hoe regularly. Thin outdoor sown seedlings when about 3 cm (1 in) high, spacing plants singly 25 cm (10 in) apart. Some of the dwarf varieties are grown closer. Prick out seeds sown in containers to 5 cm (2 in) apart in seed trays of potting compost and leave under cover. Handle seedlings by their leaves with care as they bruise easily. Harden off and plant outside 25 cm (10 in) apart with 30 cm (12 in) between rows.

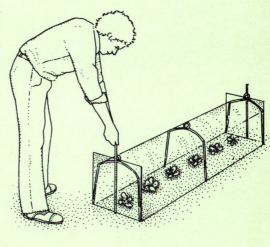

HARVESTING

Harvest in the cool of the day. Using a sharp knife, cut the stem above the lower leaves. Discard plants with a central flower shoot as they will taste bitter. For curly lettuce, simply take off leaves as required.

SPECIAL POINTS

There are two distinct types of cabbage lettuce: the quick-growing Butterheads, which are soft, smooth-leaved, hearting varieties; and the Crispheads, which are hearted, firm and crisp, taking slightly longer to mature. The cos lettuce is upright with narrow leaves of good flavour. It withstands drought better than cabbage types and is slower to mature. Some varieties form tight hearts, others need to be induced by tying in. The curly lettuce is non-hearting and forms a loose bunch of leaves. Certain varieties of curly lettuce can be picked a few leaves at a time as required over a considerable period.

Marrows and Courgettes

MARROWS need a lot of space. There are two distinct types – the bush, requiring less space and maturing earlier, and the trailing kinds which trail along the ground and need planting some 1·2 m (4 ft) apart. Courgettes produce small marrow-like fruits but the plants take up the same amount of space. However, some varieties are more compact than others and a very careful choice is needed for small gardens. These fruits are harvested from July to October.

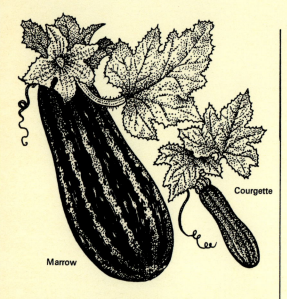

Marrow

Courgette

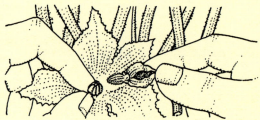

Soil: rich in humus, moisture-retentive
Site: sunny, sheltered
Sow: early sowings in April–May under glass; direct sowings into a permanent bed in May

SOWING/PLANTING

Indoors, sow singly 3 cm (1 in) deep in 8 cm (3 in) pots of seed compost. Peat pots are ideal as planting out does not disturb the roots. Germinate in cold greenhouse, frame or indoor windowsill. Harden off and plant out in May to June. To prepare the ground, take out one spit's depth where plant is to be grown or seed sown. Dig in 2–3 buckets well-rotted manure or compost into second spit. Return topsoil, forming a raised bed. Outdoors, sow 3 seeds per planting position 15 cm (6 in) apart and cover with cloches. As soon as seed leaves show, thin to one.

AFTERCARE

Control slugs. When trailing marrows have formed 4 or 5 leaves, remove the growing point to encourage 3 or 4 side shoots. Water the surrounding soil frequently. Liquid feed every two weeks. Fertilize female flowers (those with small marrows behind) by hand, if insects are not active. Pick a male flower, strip the petals and push into the open female flower, depositing pollen.

HARVESTING

Cut off young fruits with a sharp knife – courgettes at 10 cm (4 in) long and marrows at 20 cm (8 in) – to encourage heavier cropping. Protect from slugs with a board under the fruits. Near the season's end leave a few marrows to mature for store. Cut and hang in nets in a frost-free, airy place.

Mustard and Cress

THESE highly nutritious salad crops and sprouting seeds are all ready to eat within days of sowing and can be grown all the year round with ease. There is an increasing variety of sprouting seeds on the market. They are rich in proteins and vitamins. They do not depend on sun nor do they require soil or compost.

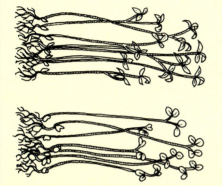

Mustard and Cress

For use together, sow cress 3–4 days in advance. Sow in warmth from September to March in a greenhouse or on a windowsill and under unheated cover between April and September. They will grow on open ground in June to August – a gamble unless covered with cloches. Make succession sowings. Sow seeds thickly on top of well moistened, sandy soil, compost or fine peat. Lightly firm the seeds but do not cover with compost. Place a piece of glass, then paper over the containers. Keep warm and moist. Remove the cover as soon as seeds germinate. Cut when the seed leaves have expanded but before the true leaves appear.

Marrows for immediate use for vegetables can be tested to see if they are tender by the ease with which you can sink a thumbnail into the skin.

Onions

ONIONS can be tricky to grow because they are susceptible to a number of pests and diseases. Growing from sets is easier than from seed. Sets are popular in colder and wet areas. However, they can bolt unless carefully watered. The quick-maturing salad onions are a useful catch crop. Shallots are grown in the same way as onions but are much easier to manage. The pickling type are quick-growing, sown thickly in spring on poorer soil and ready by July.

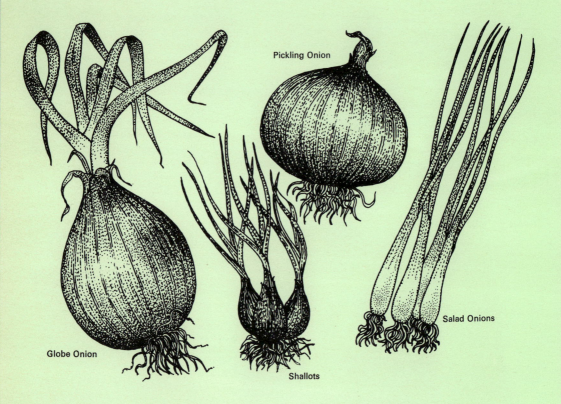

Pickling Onion

Globe Onion

Shallots

Salad Onions

Soil: deep, rich, well-worked
Site: sunny
Sow: onions – mid-August to overwinter; under cover in January; and in the open in March
Salad onions – September to overwinter; February to September
Pickling, March–April
Plant: onion and shallot sets in April; onions overwintered from autumn in March
Varieties: onions, salad onions, pickling onions and shallots

SOWING/PLANTING

Onions do well on land that has been deeply dug and well-manured in autumn and allowed to settle. In spring, lime the land if acid and work down to a fine tilth, consolidating and, before sowing or planting, rake in 100 g/m² (3 oz/sq yd) balanced fertilizer. To harvest onions in autumn, either sow under cover in January, harden off and plant out in April or sow outdoors in well-prepared drills 1 cm (½ in) deep and 30 cm (12 in) apart. A summer crop is grown from seeds sown in autumn and planted out in spring or grown from sets. Plant sets in April in a moist, well-prepared bed with drills 30 cm (12 in) apart and deep enough to cover the sets and which are 15 cm (6 in) apart. Hardy varieties of salad onions can be sown in September, in February under cloches or in open ground from March to September. Sow in 1 cm (½ in) deep drills 15 cm (6 in) apart. Plant shallots at slightly wider spacings than onion sets. Pickling onion seeds are sown thickly and can be broadcast.

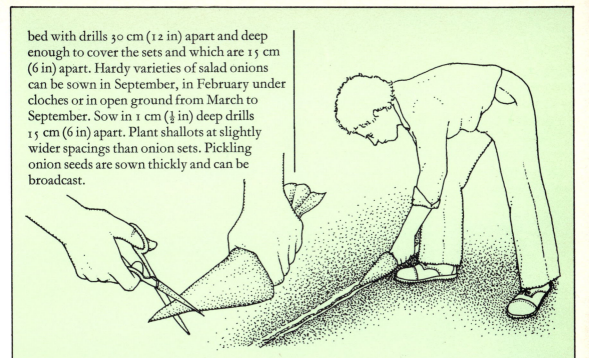

AFTERCARE

Hoe regularly, without disturbing the onions or shallots. Water well. Thin maincrop onions twice, to a final spacing of 15 cm (6 in). Remove thinnings as they attract Onion Fly. Protect from birds. Remove flower stems as they appear. When the outer leaves turn yellow, bend over the tops to help ripening. Two weeks later loosen the onions by pushing a fork underneath to sever the roots. A fortnight later, on a sunny day, fork them up and lay out to dry. Stop watering as soon as the onions begin to ripen.

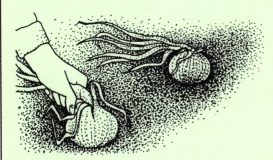

HARVESTING

When the onions have been drying for a few days cut off the tops and remove any loose scales. Store in a cool place, where air circulates. They can be laid on slatted shelves or hung up in a net. Note this is intended as a guide for averaged sized onions, some of the larger types can take up to a month to dry off fully. Harvest salad onions as they are required for use. To make a traditional 'string of onions', take a central core of string about 60 cm (2 ft) long. Bind the onions to it with string, starting at the bottom.

SPECIAL POINTS

The grubs of the Onion Fly eat into the bulbs; treat growing crop and land before sowing. White Rot is a fluffy white fungus; use fresh land. Neck Rot is a storage problem; good cultivation and feeding act as preventive measures.

Parsnips

THIS hardy crop is easy to grow, requiring little attention. It does need a long growing season, therefore work the soil as soon as possible in spring, but wait until April or May if the land is cold, sticky and wet. Parsnips provide a sweet tasting root vegetable for use in autumn and winter. Heavy or very shallow soils are generally unsuitable, although short-rooted kinds can be successful on some shallow, stony soils. Parsnips will stand over winter.

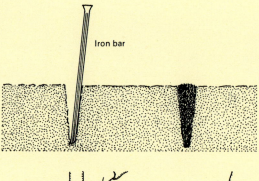

Iron bar

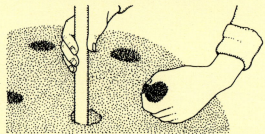

Soil: deep, well-worked, friable
Site: open, sunny, but will tolerate shade
Sow: February–May
Varieties: long-, intermediate- and short-rooted

SOWING

Use land which has been well manured for a previous crop. Fresh manure encourages root forking. Dig the land in autumn and leave rough until sowing time. As soon as the land is dry enough to work, fork down to a fine tilth and lime, if the soil is acid. Allow a few days to elapse before raking in 100 g/m² (3 oz/sq yd) of balanced fertilizer. The aim is to create a deep, reasonably dry and crumbly seedbed. Sow the seeds thinly in 3 cm (1 in) deep drills spaced 30 cm (12 in) apart. On stony soil, create pockets in which to sow seeds. Make holes and fill with sifted soil or sand. Use canker-resistant varieties, if this has been a problem.

AFTERCARE

Protect from birds. Thin to 8 cm (3 in) apart when 3 cm (1 in) high. Remove alternate plants when 10–15 cm (4–6 in) high, leaving a final spacing of 15–23 cm (6–9 in). Do not replant thinnings. Hoe and keep soil loose. Water in dry weather. If Celery Fly causes small leaf blisters, spray with malathion.

HARVESTING

Parsnips are ready as soon as the leaves begin to die down but frost improves the flavour. Leave in the ground until required. In mid-November, lift a few and store in sand in a frost-free place as a safeguard.

Peas

GARDEN peas can be picked from May to October if the right varieties are grown in succession. There are two distinct types of peas, the round seeded, which are hardy and suitable for early and late sowings and wrinkled seed, with a much finer flavour, used for sowings from March onwards. Kinds vary in height from dwarf at 45 cm (1½ ft) to tall at 1·8 m (6 ft). An early sowing can be made under glass in warmth in February, hardened off, and planted out in April.

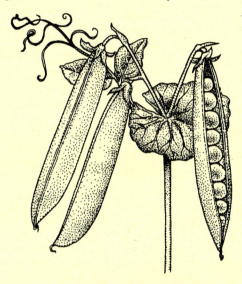

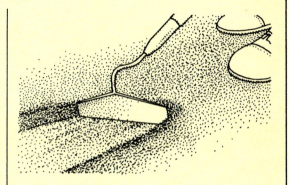

Soil: well-drained, rich
Site: sunny and sheltered from prevailing winds
Sow: March–July for summer picking; and October–November for May crop
Varieties: earlies, second earlies, maincrop and late

AFTERCARE
Protect seeds against birds with wire netting. Provide twiggy sticks as soon as growth starts and then support tall kinds with tall pea sticks or large mesh galvanized netting. Water regularly, especially when the first flowers appear and again when pods start to form. Control weeds by frequent hoeing. Watch out for mice. Cover autumn sown seeds with cloches until spring.

SOWING
Peas do well on land which has been deeply dug and manured 3–4 months before sowing. Lime the soil, if it is acid. A few days later apply 100 g/m² (3 oz/sq yd) of balanced fertilizer. Rake down to a fine tilth and take out a flat seed drill 5–7 cm (2–3 in) deep and 10–15 cm (4–6 in) wide. Space seeds 5–7 cm (2–3 in) apart. Water the drill before sowing. Cover the seeds with fine soil but do not firm. Sow a few spare at the end for gapping up. Cover the earliest sowings with cloches.

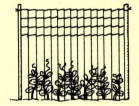

HARVESTING
Pick regularly when the pods are full but before the peas touch in the pods. Freeze any surplus to immediate requirements. Cropping is reduced if ripe pods are left unpicked. Compost the haulms and dig the nitrogen-rich roots into the ground.

Peppers

CULINARY peppers can be grown outdoors in the south and west, but they do best under glass. Chillies, cayenne and paprika which are used in curries and pickles are relatively easy to grow. The popular sweet peppers, with their blunt, round fruits, are more commonly grown. They can be used green or left on the plant to turn red. They are closely related to chillies but make a larger plant and are subject to similar ailments as those which affect tomatoes.

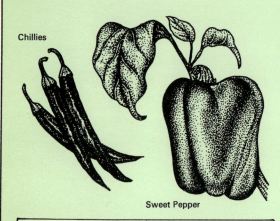

Chillies

Sweet Pepper

Soil: outdoors, rich, well-drained, fertile; indoors, No 2 potting compost
Site: sunny position against a south-facing wall or in a greenhouse
Sow: March in warmth
Varieties: culinary and decorative

SOWING/PLANTING

Sow in pots of seed compost in March at 15–18°C (59–64°F). Prick out singly into 8 cm (3 in) pots of No 1 potting compost as soon as the seedlings are large enough to handle. Hold them by the leaves. Pot on as necessary. Harden off plants for outdoor cultivation and pot indoor plants into 15–23 cm (6–9 in) pots of No 2 potting compost for fruiting. Common red or green

peppers can be planted into a greenhouse border prepared as for tomatoes, where they give a much heavier crop. Plant outdoor peppers in June against a south-facing wall on land which has been dressed with manure or compost.

AFTERCARE

Support and tie stems to canes as necessary. Syringe leaves daily during flowering period to help fruit set. Do this early in the day to give the flowers a chance to dry off before nightfall as they are subject to rotting. Give dilute liquid feed at 10 day intervals from the time the fruits start to swell until they start to show colour. Lightly shade indoor plants during hot spells. Stop peppers grown in the border at 15 cm (6 in) and allow them to grow up on two stems. Remove the side shoots. Stop at the end of July or when the plant reaches 1·2 m (4 ft), whichever is the sooner.

HARVEST

Sweet green and red peppers will be ready in August to September. Use fresh. For heavier crops, pick green to take the strain from the plant. Leave chillies on the plant until ripe in the autumn.

Potatoes

BOTH earthing up and thorough digging before planting make this a good crop for breaking up and cleaning new land. Earthing up encourages growth and the formation and spread of tubers. This, and the pre-chitting of seed potatoes, are the main features in their cultivation. Potatoes take up a lot of space so, in small gardens, grow only a few first earlies to crop when shop prices are high, or some favourite variety. Protect early crops against frost.

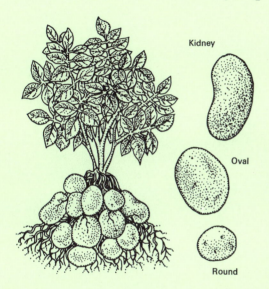

Kidney

Oval

Round

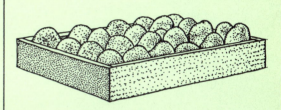

Soil: average is satisfactory; medium easily worked loam preferable
Site: open, sunny; shade encourages too much top growth
Plant: earlies, late March or mid-April in cold late frost areas; second earlies in April; maincrop in late April
Varieties: earlies, second earlies and maincrop to give succession. Available in round, oval and kidney shaped with red, yellow or white skins

PLANTING

Sprout seed potatoes before planting. In January, set out tubers in a single layer, with 'eyes' uppermost, in seed trays in a shed at 5–7°C (41–45°F), with plenty of air and some light. Aim for shoots 1 cm (½ in) long by planting time. To plant earlies, take out a drill 10–15 cm (4–6 in) deep and 60 cm (2 ft) apart. Space tubers 30 cm (12 in) apart,

shoots uppermost, in the bottom of the drill. Return soil, forming a slight ridge but do not firm. Space second earlies and maincrop 67 cm (2 ft 3 in) between rows with tubers 37 cm (15 in) apart.

AFTERCARE

To protect young shoots from frost damage, cover with fine soil or straw. Begin earthing up when shoots are 20 cm (8 in) high by breaking down the soil between rows and drawing it up to form a ridge. Earth up at

least 3 times until the plants are 30 cm (12 in) high. Spray against Potato Blight.

HARVESTING

Lift earlies in June to July, as required. Lift second earlies for use but any surplus can be stored for a short time. Harvest maincrop from September onwards for storage. Remove haulms before lifting. Dry tubers thoroughly and store in boxes in a frost-free place in total darkness or in a clamp.

Radishes

THERE are two main types of radish. The small summer kinds, used in spring and summer salads, are most commonly grown. The larger winter type, with roots up to 450 g (1 lb) in weight, is delicious sliced in salads or boiled rather like turnips. This quick-maturing crop should be grown quickly and without check to obtain crisp tender roots of fine flavour. Summer radishes are ideal to grow as a catch crop between beans, peas, lettuce or carrots.

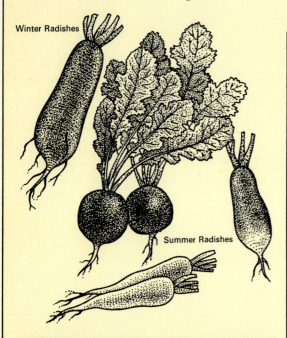

Winter Radishes

Summer Radishes

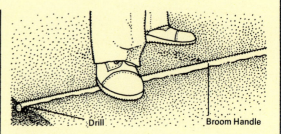

Drill   Broom Handle

before sowing. Sow thinly. Water and cover. From April to September sow in the open at 7–10 day intervals. In July and August sow in shade. Sow winter kinds in July in the north and August in the south in 3 cm (1 in) deep drills 23 cm (9 in) apart.

AFTERCARE
Dust winter kinds with derris against Flea Beetle in July. Thin to 15 cm (6 in) 4 weeks after sowing. Hoe and water regularly or

they will be hot, woody and run to seed. Protect against slugs and birds. Ventilate frame-grown crops on sunny days. Thin thickly sown summer kinds to 1 cm ($\frac{1}{2}$ in).

HARVESTING
Summer kinds are ready 4–6 weeks after sowing. Pull as needed while young and tender. Leave winter kinds in the ground until required. Cover with straw in severe weather. Ready 3 months after sowing.

Soil: well cultivated, average soil, enriched with manure and well-drained
Site: open and sunny for early and late crops; shade during mid-summer
Sow: summer radish, early March under glass; April–September in open; winter radish July–August
Varieties: summer and winter, both in round, oval and long varieties

SOWING
Dig the land, fork in peat or manure and work down to a fine tilth. Lime and a few days later rake in 70 g/m² (2 oz/sq yd) of balanced fertilizer. In February to March sow summer kinds in succession under frames or cloches in moist drills 1 cm ($\frac{1}{2}$ in) deep and 15 cm (6 in) apart. Water drills

Spinach

THREE distinct types of spinach are commonly grown. A succession of summer and winter annual varieties can be harvested all the year round. New Zealand spinach has small leaves and a branching, spreading habit. It is killed by winter frosts. Spinach beet or perpetual spinach is a kind of beet grown for its foliage. It is hardy and withstands hot summers and cold winters. The annual summer type type runs to seed unless shaded and kept moist.

Summer Spinach

New Zealand Spinach

Spinach Beet

Soil: deep, rich, moist, well-drained
Site: annual, summer, partial shade, cool; winter, sheltered, sunny; New Zealand, sunny; spinach beet, sun; light shade.
Sow: annual, summer March–July, winter mid-July–September; New Zealand, March in warmth, May outdoors; spinach beet, April for summer, July–August for winter

SOWING
Dig land and manure well in winter. Lime, if acid. Rake to a fine tilth. In spring give

140 g/m² (4 oz/sq yd) balanced fertilizer. Sow annual summer at 2–3 week intervals from March to July in 3 cm (1 in) deep drills 30 cm (12 in) apart. Sow annual winter from mid-July to late September as above. Sow New Zealand in warmth in March, harden off and plant out in May. Sow maincrop outdoors in early May, with 90 cm (3 ft) between rows. Sow spinach beet in 1 cm (½ in) deep drills 40 cm (15 in) apart.

AFTERCARE
Protect from birds. Keep watered and weed-free. Thin annual summer in two stages to 10 cm (4 in), then to 20 cm (8 in). Thin annual winter to 8 cm (3 in), then to 15 cm (6 in). Thin New Zealand to 23 cm (9 in) and spinach beet to 20 cm (8 in). Protect annual winter with cloches from mid-October. Pick out the growing points of New Zealand to encourage bushy growth.

HARVEST
Harvest annual summer from May to October. Gather largest leaves only. Harvest annual winter in October as above. Pick New Zealand leaves individually from July onwards. Pick leaves with stems of spinach beet from July onwards.

Swedes and Turnips

Wᴵᵀᴴ a careful selection of varieties, turnips can be harvested almost all year round. They should be grown quickly and, with the exception of the winter varieties, make a useful catch crop, taking only 6–8 weeks to mature. They give disappointing results on thin, sandy soils. Turnips can also be grown for their green tops – a crop sown in August gives greens in early spring. Swedes are slower-growing, hardier and keep better in the ground than turnips.

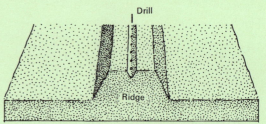

Drill

Ridge

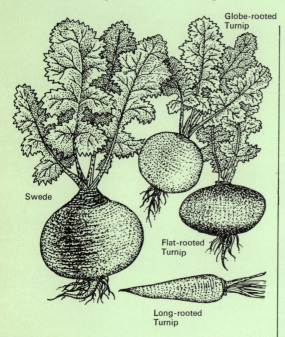

Swede

Globe-rooted Turnip

Flat-rooted Turnip

Long-rooted Turnip

turnip varieties suitable for sowing under cloches in early April are available. Sow turnips in drills 38 cm (15 in) apart. Sow swedes 45 cm (18 in) apart.

AFTERCARE

Protect from birds. Keep the ground moist and weed-free. Hoe regularly. Dust young seedlings with derris if Flea Beetle attacks, identifiable by holed seed leaves. Thin early turnips to 8 cm (3 in) when first rough leaves are formed and 3 weeks later to 15 cm (6 in). Thin maincrop turnips and swedes to 25 cm (10 in) when 3 cm (1 in) high.

Soil: deeply worked, free-draining, average, non-acid
Site: open, sunny but sheltered
Sow: early turnips April to July; maincrop turnips in late July; swedes in May or June
Varieties: turnips, globe, flat-rooted and long;
swedes, purple or bronze tops

SOWING

In wet districts or on wet land, both turnips and swedes are best grown on ridges like potatoes. These crops do well on firm ground which has been deeply worked in winter, manured for a previous crop and limed. Before sowing, rake in 100 g/m² (3 oz/sq yd) of balanced fertilizer. Early

HARVESTING

Lift earlies as required from July to October, when the size of a golf ball. Lift maincrop turnips in October to November. Twist off the tops and store in a dry, frost-free shed in layers of sand in boxes. Do not bruise the roots or they will rot. Leave swedes in the ground until required. Lift some in November and store to safeguard against the remainder being frozen.

Sweetcorn

This crop is grown for the bright, yellow cobs which are harvested from August to September until the onset of frost. They are tall plants growing to 1·35 m (4 ft 6 in). The male flowers grow at the top of the stems and the pollen falls from these to the tassled female flowers lower down, which form the edible cobs. Fertilization is by wind and cultivation aims to ensure favourable conditions for this to be effective by planting in blocks.

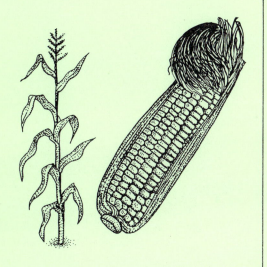

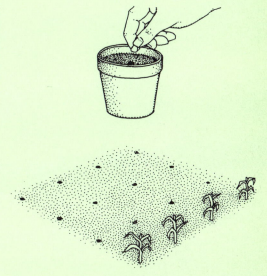

Soil : deep, fertile, moisture-retentive
Site : sunny, sheltered
Sow : mid-May outdoors in southern districts; elsewhere under glass in April
Varieties : selections suitable for warm or cool areas

SOWING/PLANTING

For best results sow seeds under glass. Sow two seeds to each 8 cm (3 in) pot of seed compost in an unheated greenhouse. Within a few days of germination, remove the weaker of the two plants. Harden off in early May and plant out at the end of May. In southern districts, sow in beds, two seeds at each station, and at similar spacings to planting. Protect with cloches. Thin to one plant after germination. Manure the growing bed well in winter. Before sowing or planting, work down to a fine tilth and rake in 100 g/m² (3 oz/sq yd) of balanced fertilizer. Plant in blocks of 12 plants with 30 cm (12 in) between plants and 75 cm (2 ft 6 in) between rows, using a trowel.

AFTERCARE

Avoid deep cultivation or the shallow roots may be damaged. Weed by hand. Keep well watered and give dilute liquid feed weekly as the cobs swell. Stake tall plants. Pinch out side shoots from the base. Keep soil up round the stems. In exposed sites draw it 15 cm (6 in) up the stems. Allow three cobs per plant to develop. In July, gently tap the stems to help pollination.

HARVESTING

Test cobs for ripeness when the silky tassels turn brown. Push a knife into 1–2 of the grains. If a creamy fluid oozes out they are ready. If watery, it is too early, if hard, too late. Gather by snapping from the main stem. Use as soon as possible after picking. Freeze any surplus.

Greenhouse Tomatoes

Tomatoes are best grown in a greenhouse. This gives the long growing season needed to ripen the fruit. A number of methods are adopted but the broad guidelines are similar. Plants can be grown successfully in greenhouse beds or borders, in growing bags and in pots of compost. Ring culture, favoured by some, involves planting the tomatoes in open ended pots of compost which are set on beds of moist aggregate. The plants are fed and watered through the aggregate.

Soil: rich loam or compost
Site: cold greenhouse
Sow: March
Plant: April
Varieties: red or yellow fruits

SOWING/PLANTING

Sow seeds thinly in pots or boxes of seed compost and cover with 6 mm (¼ in) fine compost. Cover with a sheet of glass and paper. Maintain a minimum temperature of 16°C (60°F) until seedlings appear, then remove the glass and paper. When the seed leaves have expanded, pot up the seedlings singly into 9 cm (3½ in) pots of No 1 potting compost. Place in full light. Maintain 13°C (55°F). Ventilate at 18°C (65°F), taking care not to chill the plants. Set out the plants in their fruiting positions in well-prepared and manured beds or borders into which 140 g/m² (4 oz/sq yd) balanced tomato fertilizer has been incorporated. Plant with a trowel, keeping the rootball intact. Space at 45 cm (18 in) between plants with rows 70 cm (2¼ ft) apart. Firm and water in.

AFTERCARE

Train plants up and loosely tie them to supporting bamboo canes with soft string. Remove all side shoots when small. As soon as the fruits start to swell, give liquid tomato fertilizer at weekly intervals. Keep plants well watered and avoid sudden fluctuations in moisture, feed or temperature. Remove the growing point at the second leaf above the highest truss near the top of the support. Control White Fly and remove any diseased or blotchy leaves or fruits immediately they are noticed.

HARVEST

Pick fruits as soon as they turn colour to encourage ripening and swelling of other fruits. Ripen healthy green fruits in shallow trays in a warm, dark, but well ventilated, place at 7–10°C (45–50°F).

Outdoor Tomatoes

B<small>E</small> sure to choose a variety suitable for outdoor cultivation from June to September. These are available as cordons, where one stem grows up, as dwarfs, which trail along the ground at about 15 cm (6 in) high, and as bush types, which have a drooping habit. Plants need to be purchased if a greenhouse is not available. Choose sturdy, dark green plants about 20 cm (8 in) tall and which have their seed leaves intact. Do not buy light, spindly or bluish plants.

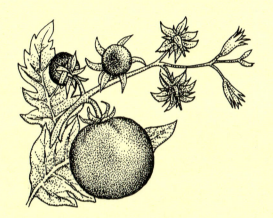

Soil: deep, rich, well-drained
Site: sunny, sheltered
Sow: in warmth in March–April
Plant: after the danger of frost has passed in late May–June
Varieties: outdoor cordons, bush or dwarfs

PLANTING

Choose a suitable site, preferably in the shelter of a south-facing wall. Some time before planting, dig the land thoroughly and deeply, incorporating a good dressing of well-rotted manure or compost. Two weeks before planting, apply a dressing of high potash base fertilizer at the rate of 100 g/m² (3 oz/sq yd). Knock the plant out of the pot, keeping the soil ball intact. Plant, using a trowel, so that the top of the soil ball is 1 cm (½ in) below the soil level. Set cordons at 45 cm (18 in) apart in rows 75 cm (30 in) apart. Plant bush and dwarf tomatoes closer together, at 60 cm (24 in). Firm in and water well.

AFTERCARE

Provide bamboo canes for cordons and, as growth is made, tie the plants to the canes loosely to allow for expansion. Control slugs. Water regularly and frequently. Irregular watering can cause the fruit to split. When the fruits have formed on the bottom truss begin to give tomato liquid feed weekly. Remove side shoots from cordons when small, rubbing out with finger and thumb or use a sharp clean knife. When four trusses have set, take out the growing point two leaves above the top truss. Dwarf and bush kinds do not need side shoots removed or stopping. During the summer give all plants at least one mulch. Lay straw under the plants as this helps to keep the lower fruits clean. It also keeps down weeds and helps to conserve moisture.

HARVESTING

Pick the fruits with the calyx still intact, as they ripen. In September, before the onset of frost, cut all the green trusses and bring indoors to ripen. Put in shallow trays and ripen in a warm, dark, but well-ventilated place at 7–10°C (45–50°F).

Irrigation and Watering

WHETHER they are grown indoors or out and regardless of how thoroughly the soil has been prepared, sooner or later seedlings and plants need watering. Well manured and mulched land needs watering less frequently than stony, impoverished ground. Although water is essential – seeds cannot germinate nor roots take up necessary nutrients without it – too much can be as harmful as too little. The method of watering varies depending on the age and condition of the crops, as well as their position and rooting medium. Watering small seedlings in pots and trays can be carried out effectively by standing the containers in trays of shallow water and soaking for 20–30 minutes or less, removing and draining as soon as the compost surface is moist. Overhead irrigation can be carried out with various kinds of sprinkler or hose. A spray attachment when using a hose pipe or a rose with a watering can avoids disturbing the soil.

WHEN AND HOW OFTEN

Water crops before they wilt. Water containers just before sowing and pricking out also, immediately afterwards and keep the compost moist at all times. If soil is very dry, apply 21 litres/m² (4½ gal/sq yd) to seedbeds 24 hours before sowing and water seed drills before sowing in dry weather. Keep seedbeds moist, watering daily in hot dry conditions. Similarly, freely water seedlings and young plants. With established leaf vegetables, like cabbage, apply 9–18 litres/m² (2–4 gal/sq yd) at least weekly; twice weekly for lettuce. With peas, beans and similar crops, defer regular watering until the pods start to swell then apply 5–9 litres/m (1–2 gal/yd) run of row twice weekly. Irrigate root crops every 2–3 weeks apply 21 litres/m² (4½ gal/sq yd).

SUITABLE APPLIANCES

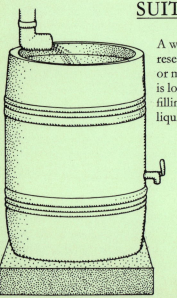

A water butt serves as a reservoir for storing rainwater or mains supply where pressure is low, saving time by pre-filling. Also useful for mixing liquid feed.

When a watering can is fitted with a fine rose, seedlings and small plants can be watered or lightly sprayed overhead to prevent wilting. Also useful for watering drills before sowing. A coarse rose is useful for watering in plants and for applying liquid feed.

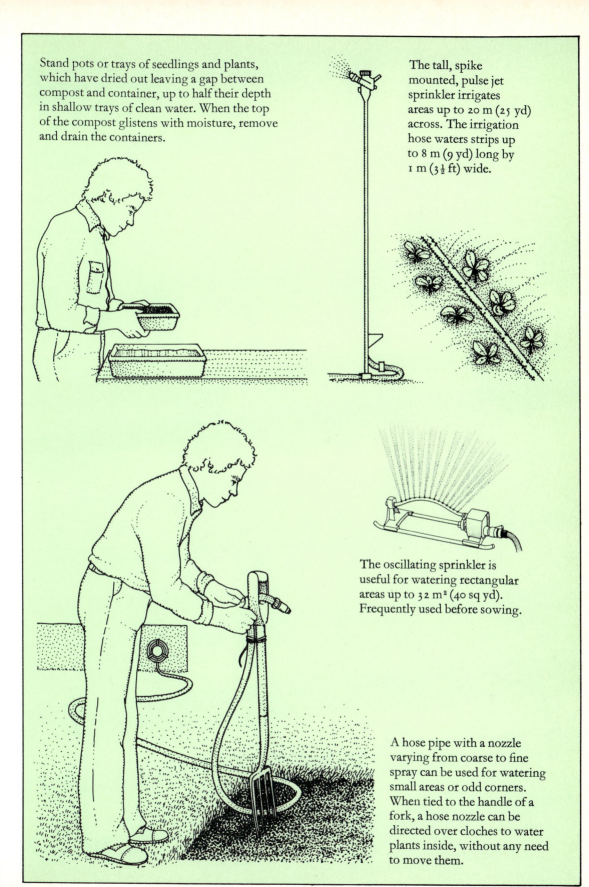

Stand pots or trays of seedlings and plants, which have dried out leaving a gap between compost and container, up to half their depth in shallow trays of clean water. When the top of the compost glistens with moisture, remove and drain the containers.

The tall, spike mounted, pulse jet sprinkler irrigates areas up to 20 m (25 yd) across. The irrigation hose waters strips up to 8 m (9 yd) long by 1 m (3½ ft) wide.

The oscillating sprinkler is useful for watering rectangular areas up to 32 m² (40 sq yd). Frequently used before sowing.

A hose pipe with a nozzle varying from coarse to fine spray can be used for watering small areas or odd corners. When tied to the handle of a fork, a hose nozzle can be directed over cloches to water plants inside, without any need to move them.

Aftercare

Heavy yields of good quality are most likely to be obtained where crops are given continued help and encouragement from sowing and planting to harvesting. Eliminate weeds by hand pulling and regular hoeing, to avoid competition for food, moisture and space. This also removes possible sources of pests and diseases. Hoeing and mulching help to conserve soil moisture in dry weather. Protect crops from bird damage and control pests and diseases with sprays, aerosols and dusts. Carry out training, staking and tying as necessary.

CONTROLLING WEEDS

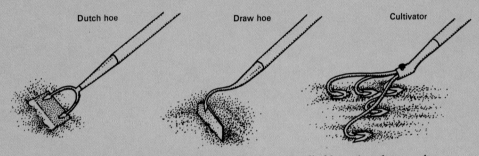

Dutch hoe   Draw hoe   Cultivator

Weeds growing among many crops can be controlled by using these tools regularly and by hand weeding in the rows. The Dutch hoe is pushed backwards and forwards to cut off weeds on average soils. The draw hoe is used with a chopping action to slash through weeds on heavy soils. The cultivator loosens the soil crust and disturbs weeds when pulled through the ground.

Mulching can assist crops and improve yields in several ways. First, it reduces loss of soil moisture through evaporation; second, it prevents capping or crust formation of the soil, allowing rainwater to penetrate freely; third, weed seedlings are smothered and unable to rob crops of valuable food and moisture.

PREVENTING CROP DAMAGE

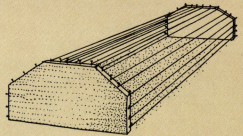

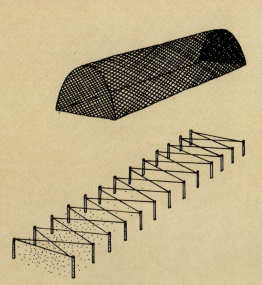

Bird damage is a main cause of lost seeds and seedlings and crop injury. Protect young crops with netting or a thread barrier. Fine mesh wire-netting tunnels are effective, provided the ends are sealed. An inexpensive method is to use black cotton tied either to rails on wooden ended frames or criss-crossed about 5 cm (2 in) above soil level tied to pegs.

The quality of summer and autumn cabbage can be much improved, especially on sandy soils, by watering, feeding and mulching when half grown.

Pest and Disease Control

SUCCESSFUL pest and disease control measures are based on preventive rather than remedial action. Applied before the outbreak of trouble, pesticides and fungicides can provide good protection, but, if action is not taken or delayed until crops are damaged, it is too late and preventing any further spread is the best that can be achieved. Good cultivation and strict hygiene combined with the timely application of chemicals offer the greatest protection for crops. Healthy, vigorous plants are better able to resist attack than weak ones. Grow pest- and disease-resistant kinds where these exist, such as the new Avon varieties of lettuce and parsnips. Buy Ministry Certified seed potatoes to start with healthy stock. Carry out crop rotation, remove any weeds, rubbish or affected plants likely to harbour pests or provide sources of infection. Use approved chemicals strictly according to the makers' directions.

10 POINT PLAN

1 Always start with healthy seeds and plants from reputable sources.
2 Use clean pest- and disease-free seed and potting composts.
3 Practise crop rotation, growing plants on fresh ground.
4 Identify any problem and use the right method to combat.
5 Remove weeds and rubbish, avoid overcrowding and provide good growing conditions.
6 Apply preventive or remedial measures in time, removing badly affected plants.
7 Mix and use approved chemicals according to the makers' instructions.
8 Apply sprays or dusts in calm, dull weather, when the leaves are dry.
9 Avoid spraying crops immediately before harvesting.
10 Clean equipment after use and store chemicals out of the reach of children and pets.

PESTICIDES AND FUNGICIDES

Name	Use
BENOMYL	Fungicide – liquid spray – all purpose
BROMOPHOS	Soil insecticide applied in granular form
CALOMEL	Soil fungicide – used as dust or liquid root dip
CHESHUNT COMPOUND	Fungicide used as pre-sowing drench for soil compost
DERRIS	Insecticide – applied as dust or spray
FENITROTHION	Insecticide – used as dust or spray
HCH	Insecticide – mainly used as dust, also given as spray
MALATHION	Insecticide – as spray or in greenhouse smokes
METALDEHYDE	Pesticide – used mainly in bait form
THIRAM	Fungicide – used as dust or spray

IDENTIFICATION CHART

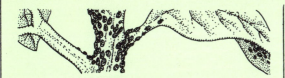

Black Bean Aphid or Dolphin Fly Symptoms: colonies of black insects mass in and around the growing point of broad beans. Control measures: remove the growing point when four flower trusses have formed. Spray affected plants with malathion.

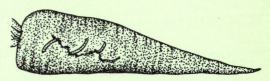

Carrot Fly Symptoms: roots holed and eaten, foliage reddening and wilting, yellowish grubs up to 6 mm ($\frac{1}{4}$ in) long present. Control measures: treat seed drills with diazinon granules. Water carrots after thinning and burn thinnings. Practise crop rotation.

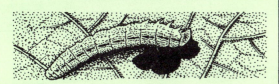

Caterpillars Symptoms: leaves, flowers and shoots holed and eaten, wrinkled greenish or brownish, sometimes striped, grubs in evidence. Can be devastating. Control measures: spray or dust affected plants with derris or fenitrothion immediately symptoms appear.

Club Root Symptoms: roots of affected plants of the cabbage family swollen, evil smelling with stunted growth. Control measures: remove and burn affected plants. Practise crop rotation. Treat planting holes with calomel or thiophanate methyl.

Grey Mould or Botrytis Symptoms: affects many crops on any part, causing rotting and soft grey mould. Control measures: cut out affected parts, remove dead plants, avoid overcrowding, ventilate indoor crops. Apply benomyl, thiram or other suitable fungicide.

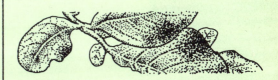

Potato Blight Symptoms: browning and rotting of leaves of potatoes and tomatoes. Tubers and fruits also affected. Control measures: apply copper spray to late potatoes and outdoor tomatoes in July. Repeat 14 days later. Earth up potatoes. Practise crop rotation.

Slugs Symptoms: seedling plants, stems and roots eaten with tell-tale silvery slime trails present. Control measures: sprinkle metaldehyde or other slug bait round young seedlings and plants regularly. Remove all rubbish and weeds likely to harbour slugs.

White Fly Symptoms: active white insects fly off many greenhouse plants, such as tomatoes, when disturbed. Plants are sickly, stunted and covered with sooty mould. Control measures: spray affected plants with malathion and repeat as necessary.

Calendar

CROP	JAN	FEB	MAR	APR	MAY	JUN	JUL	AUG	SEP	OCT	NOV	DEC
ARTICHOKE, GLOBE			◯	∘	∘		●	●	●			
ARTICHOKE, JERUSALEM	●	∘	∘	∘						●	●	●
ASPARAGUS				◎		●						
BEAN, BROAD	◯	◯	◯	◯			●	●			◯	◯
BEAN, DWARF FRENCH			◯	◯	◯	◯	◯	●	●	●		
BEAN, RUNNER				◯	◯	◯		●	●	●		
BEETROOT			◯	◯	◯		●	●	●	●		
BROCCOLI, SPROUTING	●	●		◯	◎	∘						
BRUSSELS SPROUTS	●	◯	◯	◎	∘			●	●	●	●	●
CABBAGE, SAVOY	●	●			◯	∘					●	●
CABBAGE, SPRING	●							◯	∘	∘		
CABBAGE, SUMMER	◯	◯	◯	◎	◎	∘						
CARROT	●	●					●	●	●	◯	◯	◯
CAULIFLOWER	◯		∘	◎	◯	∘	∘	●	●	●	●	●
CELERY, SELF-BLANCHING				◯		∘		●				
CELERY, TRENCH		●		◯		∘				●	●	●
CUCUMBER, GREENHOUSE		◯	◎	◎	∘	●						
CUCUMBER, RIDGE				◯	◯	∘		●	●	●		
HERBS see pages 34–37												
LAMBS LETTUCE	●	●	●	◯	◯		◯	◯	◯		●	●